This

PESTICIDES

SALLY LEE

PESTICIDES

FRANKLIN WATTS
AN IMPACT BOOK
NEW YORK LONDON TORONTO SYDNEY
1991

Photographs courtesy of: U.S. Department of Agriculture, Agricultural
Research Service: pp. 10, 21, 25, 76, 79, 82, 91, 94, 97, 98, 109,
123, 124; Sally Lee: pp. 32, 63; Coastal Fumigators, Inc.: p. 39;
National Pest Control Association:
p. 54; U.S. Fish and Wildlife Service: p. 46; Photo Researchers Inc.:
p. 51 (Kit/Max Hunn); Tracy Lee; p. 106.

Library of Congress Cataloging-in-Publication Data

Lee, Sally.
    Pesticides / by Sally Lee.
        p.   cm. — (An Impact book)
    Includes bibliogaphical references and index.
    Summary: Discusses the uses of pesticides, the dangers they may
pose to our food supply, and governmental restrictions imposed on
those considered harmful.
    ISBN 0-531-13017-7
    1. Pesticides—Juvenile literature.   2. Pests—Control—Juvenile
literature.   3. Pesticides—Environmental aspects—Juvenile
literature.   4. Pesticide residues in food—Juvenile literature.
[1. Pesticides.]   I. Title.
SB951.13.P47   1991
363-17'92—dc20   90-46839   CIP   AC

CONTENTS

PESTICIDES

PESTICIDES:
PAST AND PRESENT

In the spring of 1889, the town of Medford, Massachusetts, was covered with a blanket of crawling caterpillars, the larva of the gypsy moth. The ugly invaders coated the sidewalks, the trunks of trees, and the tops and sides of houses. Pedestrians slid on caterpillar masses that clotted the sidewalks, and ran through a rain of caterpillar droppings. The townspeople battled against their enemy as best they could. Some swept caterpillars into piles, poured kerosene over them, and set them on fire. Others collected them in burlap bags tied around the trunks of trees. By the time the creatures finally disappeared, the town's valuable fruit and shade trees had been completely stripped of their leaves. As a result, many of the trees died.

This is only one of the many times when insects have taken the upper hand in their conflict with man. In biblical times as well as today, plagues of locusts have suddenly appeared, blackening the sky with their numbers and devouring all plant life in their path. Fear of this type of destruction

In order to satisfy their voracious appetites, gypsy moths feed on plants that are useful to humans. A serious infestation of gypsy moths can leave trees completely stripped of their leaves.

makes farmers and others look for ways to do away with all pests. It is an impossible job.

EARLY HISTORY OF PESTICIDES

People have been competing with pests for food since the beginning of agriculture some 8,000 years ago. They have always had to share their crops with insects, birds, rodents, and other animals that arrived on the earth long before man. There have always been diseases to spoil crops or weeds to crowd them out.

Early methods of pest control depended on nature and hard work. The Chinese used ants to control the leaf-eating insects attacking their fruit trees. Fruit growers even built bridges of bamboo poles to help the ants travel from tree to tree. Even the early insecticides were made from natural ingredients. The crushed petals of the pyrethrum, a type of chrysanthemum, have probably been used since ancient times to kill unwanted insects, and are still widely employed in insecticides today.

Farmers have historically been plagued by pest problems and have tried a variety of techniques. Before chemical pesticides became popular, they used scarecrows and traps to discourage the larger pests. They pulled weeds by hand and picked off leaves or buds infested with insects. Others used scare tactics: To get rid of grasshoppers, whole towns marched through the fields waving their arms or sticks while shouting or beating drums. This approach was used throughout colonial times in America and is still used in some rural areas of Africa.

Some of the things farmers did in the prepesticide era probably helped control pests even though they were not thought of as pest control measures. These included rotating crops and planting a variety of crops. The fact that most farms were small and diversified may have also been helpful in controlling certain pest problems.

11

In the 1800s people began using chemicals to kill some of the pests destroying crops. Winemakers in Bordeaux, France, began spraying a mixture of lime, copper sulfate, and water on their grapes. Called the "Bordeaux mixture," this insecticide protected the grapes from fungi and insects called leafhoppers. Another chemical insecticide, Paris green (copper acetoarsenite), was also used in French vineyards and later in the United States against the Colorado potato beetle.

Slowly, more chemical pesticides were discovered and put into use. Some of these had dangerous components, such as the arsenic used on the Colorado potato beetle and the copper and mercury compounds used for disease control. But in spite of the addition of these newer compounds, progress in the area of pesticide development was slow. By the beginning of World War II there were only about thirty pesticides in use.

THE DDT ERA

In 1939 a Swiss chemist named Paul Müller was searching for something that would repel the moths eating holes in clothing. He stumbled on a chemical called dichloro-diphenyl-trichloro-ethane, better known as DDT. The chemical had been around since 1874 but no one knew that it would work as an insecticide. Müller discovered that DDT quickly killed flies. This was an important discovery because during World War II both the Allies and the Axis powers were having problems with diseases spread by flies and mosquitoes. After Müller's discovery, both sides began producing DDT to protect their people from these illnesses.

DDT's first major accomplishment was to eliminate a typhus epidemic in Naples in 1943 by killing the lice that spread the disease. DDT was also credited with saving millions of lives in Greece, Ceylon, and other countries by killing the mosquitoes that spread malaria.

DDT was viewed as a miracle. Not only did it stop the

spread of many diseases, it also killed many of the insects destroying crops and affecting people. The chemical had many advantages. It was inexpensive, easy to make, and very effective against a wide variety of pests. DDT was so good that people thought it was the final solution to all insect problems. Paul Müller won a Nobel Prize in 1948 for his discovery.

PESTICIDES AFTER WORLD WAR II

The technology of World War II provided a flood of new chemicals that were supposed to improve life. Among these were stronger insecticides, such as parathion, which was originally developed as an agent for chemical warfare by Nazi scientists. When peace was achieved, the chemicals used during the war became useful in the battle against pests. People became caught up in a pesticide frenzy. The "miracle" synthetic pesticides were so quick and easy that most other means of pest control were abandoned.

Although synthetic pesticides are still a necessary part of today's agriculture, it is now known that they are not as miraculous as was once believed. In spite of repeated applications of the chemicals, the pests still come back. Some insects have built up a resistance to many of the insecticides. In other cases there have been serious outbreaks of different insects that had not been a problem before pesticides were used.

SILENT SPRING

At first, most people were too excited about the benefits of the new pesticides to consider any potential dangers involved in their use. But Rachel Carson, a marine biologist, felt that something was terribly wrong with spraying tons of poisons over the earth with so little thought to the possible consequences. She spent four years researching the effects of

13

pesticides and herbicides on humans and the environment. Much of her information was given to her secretly by a few scientists in the U.S. Department of Agriculture (USDA) and other government agencies. These people also were worried about the effects of pesticides and herbicides on the environment, but they couldn't speak out for fear of losing their jobs.

Rachel Carson was not totally against pesticides, but felt that they were being used thoughtlessly, without consideration for their effects on soil, water, wildlife, and man. Instead of the word *pesticide*, she used the term *biocides* (life killers) because they killed much more than pests.

The publication of *Silent Spring* in 1962 put Rachel Carson at the center of a controversy. The chemical and agricultural industries accused her of basing her book on emotions instead of scientific facts. The pesticide industry thought she was ignoring the benefits of their products, benefits that had resulted in an increase in food production and a decrease in the spread of certain diseases. At least one pesticide company even tried to stop publication of the book.

In spite of all the resistance, *Silent Spring* went on to become a best-seller that was eventually translated into twelve languages. It is considered to be one of the most influential books of the twentieth century because it changed the views of so many people about pesticides. As more facts became known, the government finally had to admit that there were some dangers in pesticide use, and went on to formulate stricter regulations.

Rachel Carson died of cancer two years after her book was published. She didn't live to see DDT almost totally banned in the United States at the end of 1972, or to see the great mass of evidence building up to support her case against long-lasting biocides. In the early 1960s, several studies revealed that DDT had moved through air and water to contaminate the entire earth. DDT was found in various ocean animals and in the bodies of Antarctic penguins, even though pesticides had never been used in their habitat.

PESTICIDES IN WAR

During World War II chemists researched the possibility of using herbicides, or plant killers, to destroy Japanese food crops and eventually weaken that country. They theorized that 20,000 tons of the herbicide 2,4-D could destroy the entire Japanese rice crop. Fortunately for the Japanese, the war ended before this method could be used. However, the practice of using herbicides as war weapons became common during the war in Vietnam in the 1960s. The strong chemicals could strip the trees and bushes of their leaves, a process called *defoliation*. This had the double purpose of depriving the Vietcong guerrillas of their jungle hiding places and also of destroying their food plantations.

The most heavily used herbicide in Vietnam was Agent Orange, named for the color-coded orange strip around the drums carrying the chemical. This mixture of the herbicides 2,4,5-T and 2,4-D was a much stronger form of the chemicals used in the United States for weed and brush control. Agent Orange worked so well against the thick jungle foliage that in some areas there was a 90 percent drop in guerrilla ambushes. The practice continued for nine years until it was ordered stopped in 1971. It was later found that much of the herbicide contained dioxin, a highly toxic chemical created during its manufacturing process.

The use of Agent Orange in Vietnam is still surrounded by controversy. Some 35,000 Vietnam veterans blame the defoliant for a variety of injuries and illnesses, including a higher rate of certain types of cancer among the veterans and an increase in birth defects in their children. Government agencies, however, contend that there is no evidence to link Agent Orange to these cases. In April 1990, researchers from the U.S. Centers for Disease Control (CDC) concluded a five-year study that found no evidence Agent Orange had injured soldiers in the field. Vietnam veterans disagree with the way in which the studies were conducted. The nature of the health problems associated with Agent Orange is still unclear. The controversy continues as scientists search for more conclusive answers to the Agent Orange question.

OUR CHEMICAL WORLD

The use of chemical pesticides continues to be deeply embedded in agricultural practices. Today, agriculture is the world's largest industry, with assets worth well over $1 trillion in the United States alone. Each American farmer feeds 116 people worldwide, 86 in the United States and 30 elsewhere. With more people to feed worldwide, it has become increasingly important to improve and increase food production. Many farmers feel that chemical pesticides help to achieve this goal. As a result, the United States is the world's top producer, and user, of pesticides. According to the U.S. Environmental Protection Agency (EPA), use of all types of pesticides in the United States has more than doubled in the past twenty years, to about 820 million pounds (372 million kg) annually. Worldwide, pesticide use has skyrocketed to more than 4 billion pounds (1.8 billion kg) each year. Yet in spite of all the chemicals being dumped on our earth, the dream of having a world free of pests has never materialized.

A WORLD OF PESTS

Pests are simply living things that happen to live where we don't want them to. They are considered pests because they harm our health, eat our food, and destroy our property. Some animal pests, such as rats and mice, eat food needed for people or other animals. Other pests are viruses or fungi (molds) that damage food being grown or stored. Some pests are weeds that compete with the plants we value for sunlight, water, and minerals. By far the most abundant group of pests are insects.

There are actually only a few living things that can be considered pests, but they do a tremendous amount of damage. Experts estimate that up to a third of the food grown each year in the United States is eaten or destroyed by insects, rodents, molds, bacteria, viruses, and weeds. The figure is much higher for underdeveloped countries, which do not have the means for controlling their pests. Obviously, one way to increase our food production is to protect the food that is already grown.

In undisturbed settings, nature maintains a balance between plants and their pests. Each type of pest has its own natural enemy that keeps it in check. Large outbreaks of pests do happen in nature when the conditions are just right for fostering a population explosion, but even these outbreaks are eventually brought under control in natural ways. But when humans change this natural environment, they upset the delicate balance of nature and create more problems for themselves.

INSECTS

Compared to insects, humans are newcomers to the earth. As a group, insects are the oldest and most numerous animals that have ever evolved. Their fossils have been found in rocks more than 300 million years old. Insects have survived the radical changes that have taken place on the earth through geologic time—changes that have destroyed other more advanced forms of life. Insects' very numbers make them a force man must contend with. There are over 1 million species of insects, which means that roughly 75 percent of all the animal species on earth are insects.

Not only are there more types of insects than any other type of living creature, but most of these insects have the ability to reproduce at a fantastic rate. The champion egg layer is probably the termite, who can produce about 150 million eggs during her life. The average female housefly can produce 720 eggs during her lifetime of two or three weeks. Taking into consideration future generations, one pair of flies can produce millions more during just one summer.

Humans like to think of themselves as the lords of the land, with enough intelligence to overcome anything. But in all their years of trying, they have not been able to eliminate even one insect species or to oust the insects from their fields. The best humans have been able to do is temporarily reduce the numbers of insects in certain areas. But when this happens, other species of pests often come in to take their place.

In some ways humans are making things easier for insect pests. Farms producing a variety of crops have been replaced by *monocultures*, large areas specializing in a single crop. It is easy to see that if cornfields extend in an unbroken line from farm to farm over several miles they provide a virtual feast for corn-eating insects. This massive food supply allows these pests to reproduce at higher rates, and they then become a serious problem for farmers. Monocultures attract only a few species of insect pests, but their populations become extremely large. This contrasts with diversified agriculture, in which individual farmers grow a variety of crops, thus disrupting some pest cycles. These farms may attract a wider variety of pests but they are in smaller, more manageable numbers.

Humans are also responsible for giving pests a free ride to areas where there are no natural enemies. As settlers moved from one part of the country to another, or even across the ocean, they often carried their favorite foods and plants with them. Unfortunately, they unwittingly took along the pests of their favorite crops while leaving the pests' natural enemies behind. Without their enemies to keep them in check, the pests were able to flourish. Quite often, pests that were of little importance in their native region became serious threats in areas they had been brought to accidentally. The transplanted crops were left defenseless against the rapid population explosion of these pests. Some of the most serious pests of our times essentially hitchhiked into the areas they later damaged. Even with stricter rules requiring all plants and agricultural products to be quarantined before entering a country, pests still manage to sneak in. Each year an estimated eleven new immigrant species take up residence in the United States; seven of these will become pests of some importance.

Insects play such an important role in our lives because

they eat so much. This becomes a problem only when they compete for the food that would normally feed man and other animals. Even though a single insect may eat only a tiny bit, when this amount is multiplied by the billions of insects in the fields, the total becomes significant.

The amount of damage caused by a relatively few species of insects has caused many people to think that all insects are bad. In reality, most are not pests. It is estimated that only about 1 percent of the 1,250,000 insect species known to science are pests. In the United States there are an estimated 100,000 species of insects. Of these only about 600 are considered serious pests.

Many insects are beneficial. Bees, wasps, butterflies, flies, and other insects provide an important function by pollinating the flowers that provide us with fruits and vegetables. Bees are so valuable in carrying pollen among the blossoms of fruit trees that orchardists often rent hives and set the bees out among their trees at blossom time. Other insects are needed to keep down the populations of damaging pests. Still others provide commercial products such as honey, wax, and silk. And others are necessary links in the food chain, feeding fish and other animals.

LIFE CYCLES

Insects go through several stages during their lifetimes. Since some can do more damage at some stages than at others, it is important for those trying to control a particular insect to understand its life cycle.

Most insects lay eggs, but what happens after those eggs hatch depends on the species of insect. Some species go through *complete metamorphosis* and develop in four separate stages: the egg, the larva, the pupa, and the adult. The egg hatches into the larva, usually a caterpillar, which spends its time eating and growing. This stage is usually the most

*A very small percentage of the insects
that share our planet is considered
pests. Among the helpful insects
is the lady beetle, or ladybug,
which eats hundreds of damaging aphids.*

destructive to plant life. When the caterpillar is grown, it becomes a pupa inside the cocoon, or pupal case, it has made. While in the pupa stage, the insect undergoes internal changes, then emerges as an adult moth or butterfly that mates to produce the eggs for the next generation.

Other insects, such as grasshoppers and dragonflies, go through an *incomplete metamorphosis*. Most of them have three stages: egg, larva or nymph, and adult. The nymphs are just tiny versions of the adult. In order to grow, the insect molts, shedding its hard outer skeleton and getting a new and larger one.

WEEDS

Weeds are merely plants that grow where they are not wanted. They can be a problem for gardeners and farmers because weeds take their share of the sunlight, water, and soil nutrients needed for more valuable plants. They also can harbor pests and plant diseases that could damage the more desirable plants.

On a larger scale, weeds can be expensive because of the damage they do to crops. At one time they were a big problem for the railroad and utility companies. Tough weeds grew up between the tracks and interfered with trains. Weeds that grew under power and telephone lines created problems in the power transmission and telephone impulses.

But even weeds are not all bad. Some of them excrete odors that repel harmful insects. Others can destroy harmful bacteria. Deep-rooted weeds can break up hard soil so that the roots of beneficial plants can grow deeper. This aeration also allows more air and water into the soil. Many of the deep-rooted weeds pull minerals from the subsoil to the surface, making these minerals more accessible to other plants. Other weeds provide food for people or animals. Still others protect the ground as a cover crop, preventing it from blowing away and then adding their organic matter to it.

DISEASES

As in all other living creatures, plants can be killed or damaged by diseases. Before the middle of the nineteenth century, no one knew what caused diseases in plants. Some blamed them on "evil fogs," wind, excess moisture, nutrition, insects, or other factors. In 1860, Louis Pasteur, a French chemist known primarily for his work on fermentation, pasteurization of milk products, and preventive vaccines, finally proved that the microorganisms found in diseased or decaying tissues came from living things. By 1900 scientists had accepted the belief that bacteria could cause diseases. Viruses were also recognized as disease-causing agents, but they were so small that it was difficult to study them until the electron microscope was invented in the early 1930s.

There are two types of diseases. Those that are caused by living things are called *biotic*, or pathogenic, diseases, and are caused by parasites or other living microorganisms. These diseases are often aided by environmental factors. Most diseases develop best in warm, moist conditions, which explains why there are fewer parasitic diseases in plants grown in the dry western states than in those grown in humid climates.

When diseases are caused strictly by environmental factors, without any living microorganisms involved, they are called *abiotic*. They may be produced by air pollution, lightning, chemical spray burn, or too much or too little of a particular mineral in the soil.

FUNGI

Fungi are a group of very simple plants that do not contain chlorophyll, the compound that makes leaves green. They occur everywhere in water, soil, and air. Fungi cannot manufacture their own food, so they must exist on live or dead plants or animals. Those that live and feed on living plants or animals are called *parasitic* fungi. Those that feed on dead plant and animal matter are called *saprophytic* fungi.

Parasitic fungi are the most harmful. They include rusts, mildews, and mold, which can destroy many useful plants. One of the most disastrous results of fungi was the Irish potato famine of 1845. It destroyed the potato crop in Ireland, causing a million people to starve to death and another million to immigrate to the United States.

Not all fungi are bad. Saprophytic fungi are necessary for decomposing organic matter. Without them, the world would become encumbered with the remains of dead animals and plants. Fungi such as yeasts, some mushrooms, and truffles can be eaten. Still others are used in medicines. And some fungi, such as certain molds, can be used to protect plants from damaging diseases.

NEMATODES

Nematodes are nearly invisible worms that are on nearly every American fruit, vegetable, and grain crop. The most damaging group, known as *plant parasitic nematodes*, do an estimated $5 billion worth of damage to U.S. crops every year. The most damaging is the "root-knot" nematode, which is found in more than 1,700 host plants and covers most of the vegetables, nursery crops, field crops, nuts, fruits, and vines grown in this country. The larvae of the root-knot nematode invade the roots of plants and prevent them from growing longer. Then the nematode injects a substance into the plant that causes certain cells to swell. The nematode feeds on these giant cells, disrupting the plant's ability to take in food and water. Eventually, the root system shrinks and the plant's growth deteriorates, which results in a reduced yield for the crop.

The damaging root-knot nematode, shown here magnified 1,800 times, causes stunted growth in a large variety of plants.

WILDLIFE

All wildlife species have both positive and negative aspects. At times they are bothersome to humans because they eat our plants and may also spread diseases. Some types of wildlife are more bothersome than others. Although birds may cause some problems by damaging fruits and raiding berry patches, they are typically more beneficial than harmful because of the harmful insects they eat. This cannot be said for many rodents and other warm-blooded animals.

Perhaps the most damaging group of animals are rodents, especially rats and mice. Rodents consume, contaminate, and cause extensive damage to agricultural crops. It is said that for every two dollars' worth of food they eat, they cause twenty dollars' worth of damage. Rats feed on garbage, meat, fish, cereal, grain, and fruits. They can spread diseases by contaminating food with excrement and other filth. The fleas they carry can also transmit diseases to humans.

Small mammals, such as chipmunks, ground squirrels, moles, gophers, and shrews, eat a large number of seeds. Rabbits are responsible for damage to young trees, vegetable crops, and grain fields, as well as home gardens and ornamental plants. They can also strip the bark from established orchard trees.

Whether in the form of insects, weeds, diseases, wildlife, or a number of other forms, pests are here to stay. We will never be able to do away with them. All we can do is attempt to limit the amount of damage they do.

PESTICIDES:
CLASSIFICATION
AND CONTROL

In World War II it was not only human enemies that the soldiers on both sides had to worry about. They also faced a deadly threat from the diseases common in the tropical climates where many of the battles took place. Doctors knew that lice carrying typhus disease had often caused more fatalities during wars than the actual conflicts themselves. A breakthrough came when it was discovered that DDT would kill the offending insects.

In addition to saving thousands of lives during World War II, DDT was used in agriculture to combat a variety of insect pests damaging crops and livestock. DDT's spectacular success both in war and in agriculture stimulated a mushrooming pesticide industry that continues to grow even today.

In many languages, the word for pesticide translates as "medicines for food." In our language, the word simply means things that will kill pests. There are many different kinds of pesticides named for the type of pest they are designed to kill. There are insecticides to control insects, fungicides to control fungi such as mold and mildew, herbicides to control weeds, and rodenticides to control rodents such as rats and mice. There are also nematocides to control the tiny worms called nematodes that are harmful to plants.

INSECTICIDES

Since insects are man's most damaging pests, insecticides make up the largest share of pesticides. There are many different kinds of insecticides, each with its own ingredients and its own method for bringing death. Stomach poisons kill insects that have chewing mouthparts. These insecticides may be sprayed or dusted directly on the insect's food or may be mixed with baits to attract the pests. These poisons must kill quickly because the insect is already doing damage when it ingests the insecticide.

Contact insecticides kill on contact. They are sprayed or dusted directly on pests or are spread where pests will pick them up. They are especially useful in controlling insects with piercing-sucking mouthparts. When these insecticides are eaten, they become stomach poisons. Most of the common insecticides we buy in stores and nurseries are contact insecticides. Whether they act as stomach poisons or kill on contact, insecticides are further classified by their chemical makeup.

Inorganic Insecticides: Inorganic insecticides contain no carbon in their chemical structure. They include heavy metals, such as arsenic, mercury, zinc, and thallium, and nonmetals such as sulfur, boron, and fluorine. In the late 1800s a few inorganic insecticides, such as the Bordeaux mixture and Paris green, came into use. In addition to combatting pests in the vineyards of France, and the Colorado potato beetle in the U.S., Paris green was later used against grasshoppers so successfully that orchardists adopted it in their fight to control codling moths on apples and pears.

By the 1860s many chemical formulations, usually prepared by the farmer, were in use. The active ingredients were compounds of arsenic, mercury, selenium, sulfur, thallium, or zinc. These chemicals were dangerous and left poisonous residues on the plants. For example, not only did the heavy use of lead arsenate in apple orchards injure the foliage and fruit, but after years of heavy spraying the trees themselves were injured and the soil poisoned.

Fuel oil and kerosene were also among the early pesticides used in this country. Oils are still useful both as carriers for insecticides and as insecticides themselves. Dormant oils are sprayed on trees and shrubs during the late winter or early spring before their foliage grows. These dormant oils work by suffocating pests such as scales, mites, eggs, and some larvae. Unless chemicals are added, these oils are not poisonous to warm-blooded animals.

Organic Insecticides: Organic insecticides are compounds containing chains of carbon and hydrogen atoms (hydrocarbon). They can be separated further according to their source. *Botanicals*, or natural organic insecticides, are produced by plants. Manufactured compounds are called *synthetic organics* and include chlorinated hydrocarbons, organic phosphates, carbamates, and synthetic pyrethroids.

Botanicals: With the exception of sulfur, and later arsenic (which was first used by the Chinese in the sixteenth century), the first insecticides to be widely used were botanicals. As a rule, since botanicals are derived from plants, they are the least dangerous of the insecticides. They break down into harmless substances that will not hurt warm-blooded animals.

Some botanicals have been used for hundreds of years. Nicotine, derived from tobacco plants, was in common use as an insecticide in the eighteenth century. White hellebore, which comes from a type of lily, was used against aphids in France as early as 1787. Rotenone was extracted from the *Derris* plant and put into modern use in the 1920s. But the most successful of all the organic insecticides is pyrethrum, which comes from the pyrethrum flower, a member of the chrysanthemum family.

Today, new plants are being looked at to expand the range of natural pesticides. Some of these plants can grow in arid regions that are too dry for the production of traditional crops. The most promising of these newer botanicals come from the neem tree. Extracts from the seeds of neem trees affect the feeding habits of some insects, inhibit the growth and development of others, and render others unable to reproduce.

Chlorinated hydrocarbons: DDT was the first chlorinated hydrocarbon insecticide. Its spectacular success prompted the development of several more of this type, including chlordane, lindane, and heptachlor. These insecticides were considered miracle workers when they were first developed because of their success in killing a wide range of insects. They were very popular from 1945 through 1960 because they were inexpensive, killed a wide variety of insects, and, at that time, were not considered to be particularly dangerous to workers applying them. By 1960 the United States was producing 163 million pounds (74 million kg) of DDT a year. By that time it was estimated that more than 4 billion pounds (1.8 billion kg) of DDT had been produced around the world.

One advantage of the chlorinated hydrocarbons—which later was viewed as their biggest hazard—was their persistence, their ability to last a very long time. Although persistent insecticides are convenient because they don't have to be reapplied so often, they can be more harmful to the environment because they accumulate. Instead of breaking down, or degrading, they are passed through the food chain. The chemicals may be taken in first by microorganisms that are eaten by animals, fish, or birds, which in turn may be eaten by other animals or humans. Instead of being broken down in the body, persistent insecticides tend to accumulate in the fat of each creature and become more concentrated in animals further up the food chain. Several studies suggest that exposure to these chemicals is a health risk. Even though the use of DDT was banned in the United States in 1972, traces of the chemical are still found in the body of nearly every American.

Organophosphates and Carbamates: Over a period of time, evidence began indicating that DDT and other hydrocarbons were dangerous to humans and to the environment. Amid a fair degree of disagreement and controversy, the chlorinated hydrocarbons were phased out and were replaced by a newer generation of chemicals called *organophosphates*. This group included malathion and diazinon and were considered safer because they were biodegradable, breaking down before they could contaminate the environment. However, in order to be effective they must be applied often.

Organophosphates were developed just before World War II as a result of chemical research into poisonous gases for warfare. Although they have the advantages of degrading quickly and of being more selective, killing only certain pest species while leaving beneficial insects alone, they are potentially dangerous to man and animals. Some of these chemicals are initially more toxic than the hydrocarbons such as DDT, and in some cases, the breakdown products may be more toxic than the original chemicals. Organophosphates can be taken into the body through the mouth or the skin or by inhalation of the fumes. One organophosphate, parathion, is particularly toxic to many forms of life and is considered to be a possible human carcinogen.

Organophosphates may be supplemented with a new group of insecticides called carbamates. This group of contact insecticides includes carbaryl and propoxur. Carbamates are even less persistent than organophosphates and may pose fewer health hazards to man. However, if not used correctly, they can cause local environmental problems. For example, carbaryl is particularly toxic to bees, the insects most important to the pollination of plants in the wild and on farms.

Many insecticides used today are composed of natural compounds, such as plants and flowers, natural bacteria, and insecticidal soaps instead of synthetic chemicals.

HERBICIDES

As our society became more advanced technologically, weeds became more of a problem. Farms became larger and more specialized, and often abandoned the diversified crop rotations that had helped to disrupt weed and pest cycles and maintain the health of the farm soils. Farmers began looking for easier ways to rid their fields of weeds before planting their crops. In addition, railroads and telephone and other utility companies found weeds troublesome.

Before the development of herbicides, many methods were used to try to control weeds. Fires were often set on rangelands in the Southwest to kill oak brush, which interfered with the grasses needed to feed livestock. Timbermen in the Northwest hacked, bulldozed, burned, and sprayed scrub oak and other unwanted plants that prevented pine seedlings from getting the sun and water they needed. From the late 1800s on, European farmers had been using highly caustic chemicals, such as sulfuric acid, to battle their weeds. Americans didn't like these chemicals because they were too expensive.

The earliest herbicides were not in the least selective. They killed the good plants right along with the weeds. The first effective herbicides were discovered by accident in the 1930s when scientists experimenting with growth hormones found that if they gave the plants too much of the hormone, the plants died.

Research into herbicides became secretive and more intense during World War II, when the military was looking for new methods of biological warfare. After the war, scientists could finally reveal that they had developed herbicides that could kill specific plants while leaving others unharmed. The most promising herbicide was 2,4-D, which was patented in 1945. Experiments showed that it could kill weeds and leave only pencil-sized holes in the grass. Just a small amount on a leaf would spread throughout the plant and eventually kill even the roots.

Today, weed control involves many different chemicals. Some, such as 2,4-D, are selective, killing certain weeds without harming others. Many, however, destroy all vegetation. Farmers use these to clear their fields before they plant their crops and thus do not have to plow weeds under the soil to prepare it for planting. The enthusiasm over herbicides has caused much of its misuse and, as a result, many beneficial plants have been damaged and more chemicals have found their way into the environment.

Many herbicides are toxic and have caused cancer in laboratory animals. The risk is greater for those, such as farm workers, who come in contact with large quantities of herbicides. A study made by the National Cancer Institute found that farmers exposed to herbicides had a six times greater risk than nonfarmers of contracting a particular type of cancer.

FUNGICIDES

Most chemical fungicides cannot actually kill a fungus already actively growing in a plant. Fungicides are effective only as preventive measures. As a result, fungicide users generally have to make frequent applications to prevent the problem from starting. Fungicides sprayed on plants act as a barrier to the growth of fungus. When the spores of a fungus begin to grow on a treated plant, the root of the fungus comes in contact with the chemical, which prevents it from penetrating the host plant. There are now systemic fungicides on the market that plants absorb with water to control fungal disease from within. So far, these have been somewhat effective only with fungi on certain types of plants.

Fungicides are used on many fruits and vegetables, particularly in the eastern and southeastern regions of the country. They are also used heavily on golf courses and other landscaped environments.

The necessity for frequent applications of fungicides is a cause for concern. According to the National Academy of Sciences, about 90 percent of all fungicides are considered to be potential *oncogens*—that is, chemicals capable of producing benign or malignant tumors in animals or humans. Thus, some scientists are particularly concerned about the potential for human cancer risk from exposure to these pesticides.

NEMATOCIDES

For centuries farmers had tried to find a way to get rid of the nematodes, or tiny worms, damaging their crops. The early chemicals used were flammable, poisonous, and expensive. Some of the early nematocides were chemicals used in World War I as tear gas. Another chemical, carbon disulfide, was so volatile that even the spark from a plow hitting a stone could ignite an entire field.

The first successful nematocide was discovered by accident in the early 1940s. Scientists at the Pineapple Research Institute in Hawaii were trying to save Hawaii's pineapple crop from pest devastation. These scientists applied a waste product from the Shell Chemical Company's glycerin production. Much to the researchers' surprise, the chemical not only made the plants grow better but also worked against nematodes. Shell named the chemical dichloropropane-dichloropropene, or D-D. The early nematocides had to be used several weeks before crops were planted; if they were applied after the crops were planted, the crops would be poisoned too. A nematocide was finally developed that could safely be put on plants. It could either be injected into the soil or added to irrigation water.

Nematocides pose a particularly high risk of groundwater contamination. In order to be effective in the soil zone where crop roots may be damaged by nematodes, these chemicals are designed to be mobile. Thus, they easily move into groundwater as well. Also, severe problems with nematodes often occur in sandy, porous soils, which tend to allow rapid infiltration of chemicals into groundwater.

FORMULATIONS AND APPLICATION

Pesticides are not only classified by their chemical makeup but by the way those chemicals are formulated. The toxic chemical that does the killing is called the *active ingredient.* Pesticide formulas also contain *inert ingredients* that are added to improve the physical properties or the effectiveness of the pesticide. Inert ingredients include sticking agents to improve the adherence of the pesticide to plants or soil and spreaders to allow coverage of the pesticide over the target area. Inert ingredients also contain carriers that take the active ingredients to the target area. Some widely used carriers are talc, bentonite, and diatomaceous earth.

Many pesticides are dry formulations in the form of dusts, granules, baits, and wettable or soluble powders. In dusts, the active ingredient is mixed with clay or some other dry carrier. Dusts have some drawbacks because they do not always stick to the target surfaces and can be carried by the wind to other areas. This increases the hazards to the environment and to the person applying the pesticide. Granules are made up of larger dry particles. They are easy to apply and don't drift as readily as dusts. Granules are an effective means of applying insecticides to the soil to control insects that feed on the parts of plants growing beneath the ground. Two of the other dry formulations, wettable and soluble powders, are mixed with water prior to application.

Other pesticides are formulated as liquids. Most of the liquids use water as their carrier, although oils and other formulations are also used. Oil formulations are unusual because oil is both the active ingredient and the carrier. Some concentrated oil solutions are mixed with an emulsifier, such as soap, which breaks the oil down into tiny droplets to enable the concentrate to mix with water for spraying.

Fumigants are poisonous gases or liquids with low boiling points that kill insects in enclosures, such as buildings or containers, in the soil, or under temporary covers such as tarpaulins and tents. Fumigants have the advantage of penetrating into all parts of the enclosed area in order to reach all insects. They leave no residue. Fumigants are often used in warehouses and mills for destroying insects in stored grain, dried fruit, and nuts. Fumigants may be effective but they are also dangerous. Some are explosive, and most are more poisonous to humans than to insects. For safety reasons, some fumigants are mixed with a small amount of tear gas so workers will know whether they are too close to the spray or are using too much for a particular enclosure. They should be used with extreme care and only under controlled circumstances by qualified pest-control operators.

Aerosols are pressurized mixtures of chemicals in a propellant. The active ingredient is mixed with a liquefied gas. The vapor pressure of the gas serves as the propellant, forcing the insecticide through a small tube. The spray leaves small droplets of insecticide on the target surfaces. All aerosol products probably contain some carcinogenic chemicals and are thought to be damaging to the earth's ozone layer. Pump sprays are a safer alternative.

THE FAILURE OF PESTICIDES

At first pesticides were seen as miracle workers. Pests were dying. Epidemics of malaria and typhus were being stopped. Crops were being saved. Then entomologists discovered that the problems they thought they had solved were returning. Some species of insects that had been eliminated began reappearing, sometimes in even larger numbers. New insects, which had not been a problem earlier, became serious pests. Clearly, the pests had some tricks of their own.

Pest resurgence. One reason chemical warfare against pests has not been entirely successful is due to the phenomenon of pest resurgence. This occurs when the very pests that have been killed by pesticides return in even larger numbers. This happens because the chemicals not only kill the pest insects but also do away with the natural enemies that eat the pests and keep their numbers down. The natural enemies either are killed by the insecticide or leave the area because there is no longer any food.

Insects, whether pests or beneficial, are not going to go where there is no food. Once insecticides are used, the pests may be removed temporarily but the food supply is still there to lure them back. The pests' natural enemies are not going to return until the pest population is sufficiently large, which gives the pests an opportunity to reproduce rapidly because there are no natural enemies to limit their numbers. The result is a powerful resurgence of the pest.

Pest resistance. In the early 1960s, DDT was used in the Asian country of Sri Lanka to control mosquitoes carrying malaria. The DDT worked wonders. By 1966, there were only seventeen cases of malaria in Sri Lanka. But by 1970 there were an estimated 4 million cases. The disease-carrying mosquitoes had built up a resistance to DDT—the chemical no longer affected them.

Not all insects are killed during the application of an insecticide. Some may receive such a small dose that they survive. Others are just naturally more resistant to the chemical. When these surviving insects reproduce, they pass their resistance on to the next generation. Most insects reproduce at a phenomenal rate so that before long, large numbers of the insects are resistant to the poisons. Over a few years, an entire population that is unaffected by the pesticides evolves. Frequent applications of the poison speed up this process. If a stronger dose or another chemical is used, the process starts all over again. By the end of 1986, close to 500 insect species

*A tent is placed over dwellings, such
as this house, to keep in the fumigant,
or poisonous gas, that is being used
to kill the insects inside.*

were reported to be resistant to at least one pesticide group, with 17 species resistant to all insecticides.

When insects become resistant to one pesticide, they may also be resistant to another pesticide that is chemically similar, even when that pesticide has never been used in their area. This is called *cross-resistance.* It is even more serious when pests develop *multiple resistance*, or resistance to several classes of insecticides. Some species are resistant to every chemical used against them. Today, pest control specialists often rotate different classes of insecticides with different modes of action and different chemical classes. Since the insects respond to these different insecticides in different ways, they are less likely to develop resistance to them.

Secondary pests. Sometimes after the widespread application of a pesticide, a new species of pest, which may have been unnoticed before, suddenly becomes a problem. Farmers trade one insect enemy for another that may be even worse. For example, spider mites have become almost a worldwide problem since DDT and other insecticides have killed so many of their natural predators, such as ladybugs, which are sensitive to insecticides. With many of its enemies eliminated, the spider mite, which seems unaffected by the pesticides, can reproduce in much greater numbers.

When a person who has applied an insecticide sees an even larger population of insects, the natural reaction is to spray more often or to use stronger, more deadly chemicals. When this triggers still another outbreak of pests, the person sprays again. This puts into motion an *insecticide treadmill* in which repeated pest outbreaks encourage further spraying, which, in turn, creates more serious outbreaks.

GOVERNMENT CONTROLS OF PESTICIDES

The United States government began regulating pesticides as far back as 1910, when the Federal Insecticide Act was passed. Its main function was to protect farmers against weakened or mislabeled products. This also served to protect the more reputable manufacturers whose fledgling sales efforts suffered when farmers were defrauded by worthless pesticides.

In 1947 the government increased its control over the flourishing pesticide industry with the Federal Insecticide, Fungicide and Rodenticide Act (FIFRA). It required pesticides to be registered by the secretary of agriculture before being marketed to protect users from ineffective and dangerous pesticides. Although it was a beginning, environmental science had not yet developed enough to anticipate all types of data necessary for assessing the effects of these chemicals on human health and the environment.

At first the regulation of pesticides was controlled by the Agriculture Department, which was presumably more interested in how many bushels per acre they could produce than in the potential harmful effects of the pesticides. Some complained that the Agriculture Department was not enforcing the standards set down by FIFRA. When the Government Accounting Office (GAO) looked into the matter, they found that the Agriculture Department had not enforced FIFRA until midway through 1967.

In the twenty years following the passage of FIFRA, new data became available on the potential side effects of toxic chemicals, including harm to the environment and more long-term health problems such as cancer and birth defects. In 1972 Congress added more stringent health and safety requirements, and pesticide regulation was transferred to the newly created EPA.

Pesticide makers were now required to provide data not only on the chemical's acute or short-term effects but also on its chronic, or long-term, effects. The new regulations also required the EPA to review certain data on every major chemical product registered since 1947. These new restrictions were almost impossible to enforce. The EPA could barely keep up with its current work load, much less go back

41

and reevaluate the thousands of products already on the market. Since older products are allowed to stay on the market until the EPA can test them, many of the pesticides used today have not passed the same stringent health and safety tests as the newer pesticides being registered.

The Federal Pesticide Act of 1978 was created to simplify the process of reregistering pesticides. It only required the registration of approximately 600 basic chemicals that make up the pesticide products instead of the registration of each individual product. But the act has not speeded up the process enough. A 1984 National Academy of Sciences study showed that of 3,350 pesticides and their inert ingredients, complete health hazard assessment was possible for only 10 percent. Less than minimal information was available for 64 percent of these chemicals. At the time of the study, the EPA had identified some 600 active pesticide ingredients considered to be commercially important, but only 2 of the 600 had been reregistered.

Finally, after sixteen years of attempts at compromise between the agricultural-chemical industry and environmental groups, new amendments to FIFRA were passed in 1988. The new bill gives the EPA nine years to complete testing of about 600 key ingredients used in some 50,000 pesticide products.

SHOULD PESTICIDES BE BANNED?

In order to produce the amount of food we need to feed the rapidly growing world population, we must protect that food from pests. The United Nations estimates that each year insects and weeds destroy enough crops to feed a billion people. A quarter of all the people in the world who starve to death do so because of losses to pests. Although pesticides have been important tools in food production, there exists considerable controversy over the likely impact of removing pesticides from use. Some believe that crop losses would be dramatic and that the price of food would escalate sharply. Others contend that the losses would not be too great and that food prices would stabilize over time, with the possible exception of those of certain fruits, vegetables, and specialty crops.

The foods we grow today are more susceptible to pests than those grown a hundred years ago. Our crops have been bred for high yields rather than for survival under adverse conditions. Monocultures, in which large areas are planted with a single crop, attract more pests and require more pesticides to ensure their growth. Also, we have become accustomed to having perfect-looking fresh fruits and vegetables. This requires the use of more pesticides. Thus far we have not found economical alternatives to chemical pesticides for all current uses.

In addition to protecting the world's food supply, pesticides have saved many lives by killing the insects that spread disease, such as the mosquitoes carrying malaria and yellow fever and the lice carrying typhus. Thanks to our knowledge of pesticides, people in the United States don't know what it's like to experience an epidemic caused by these insects. Pesticides have made it possible for many people to survive, particularly in the tropics. It is doubtful that the Panama Canal could have been built if it were not for pesticides, which eliminated epidemics of yellow fever and malaria so common in that area. More recently, pesticides have been used in Canada and the United States to kill mosquitoes carrying Saint Louis encephalitis.

We cannot entirely escape the chemical world we have created. The best we can do is to use pesticides selectively, combined with nonchemical means of controlling pests, some of which were employed by farmers prior to the emergence of pesticides and some of which are results of new advances in science. We must also develop the most effective pesticides that will protect our crops and keep diseases at bay, yet will not harm the environment and all living things within it.

PESTICIDES AND
THE ENVIRONMENT

Gripping their ropes tightly, two mountain climbers slid over the side of a cliff above Crater Lake in Oregon and rappelled 150 feet (46 m) down the sheer rock wall. Finally they saw their target—the nest of a peregrine falcon with four brown speckled eggs nestled inside. When they arrived at the nest, the climbers gently lifted the eggs out and put them in a specially designed case. They replaced them with four imitation peregrine eggs, then carefully made their way back up the wall. This may sound like a cruel joke on the mother falcon, but the climbers were actually saving the lives of her babies.

At one time peregrine falcons were common in America and many other countries. People marveled at their superb hunting and flying ability. The birds dove through the air, reaching speeds as high as 175 miles (282 km) an hour to catch prey several hundred feet away. For some mysterious reason, the birds began disappearing. By the mid-1960s, peregrines were 90 percent extinct in some northern Euro-

pean countries and in the western United States. East of the Mississippi River, where there had once been nearly 200 nest sites, the falcons had completely disappeared.

The mystery was finally solved. The peregrine falcons, as well as other carnivorous birds such as the bald eagle and the osprey, were ingesting heavy concentrations of DDT in the small mammals they were eating. Studies showed that DDT caused these birds to produce eggs with weak shells, or even no shells at all. As a result, fewer baby birds were being born and some species became almost extinct. Caring people began breeding some of the birds in captivity, later releasing them into the wild. Others borrowed the eggs from the nest and hatched them in incubators. They later returned the baby birds to the nest to be raised by the peregrines. Today the population of all of these birds has increased.

The near-extinction of some birds of prey is only one example of the harmful effects pesticides can have on our environment. Spreading millions of tons of poisons over the earth has touched all forms of life, including plants, insects, wildlife, and even humans.

PESTICIDE BONANZA

Before the end of World War II pesticides were used less frequently and mainly against a few key pests. But as scientists developed new products for chemical warfare, they also developed cheaper, more effective pesticides such as DDT. The war also brought an abundance of surplus airplanes that could be used to apply these new poisons over much wider

Birds of prey, such as the peregrine falcon, almost became extinct because of the buildup of DDT and similar pesticides in the food chain.

47

expanses of farmlands and forests. Eventually, everything—human or nonhuman—could be touched by what one British ecologist referred to as "an amazing rain of death."

Even while the government was testing the harmful effects of DDT and considering a possible ban on its use, the chemical continued to be used heavily. Some of the massive spraying proved to be as foolish as it was dangerous.

In the mid-1950s, the Plant Pest Control Division of the Agriculture Department set up a spraying program to eradicate the gypsy moth. The program started in 1956 with the spraying of over a million acres in Pennsylvania, New Jersey, Michigan, and New York. In spite of complaints of damage, even more spraying was done the next year. This time even the heavily populated areas of the state of New York were sprayed, even though the gypsy moth was generally not a problem in cities. The DDT mixed with fuel oil hit not only the trees with gypsy moths, but also truck gardens and dairy farms, fish ponds, suburban homes, and any people or animals who happened to be in the way. The harmful effects of the spraying showed up immediately. A horse in one New York field died ten hours after drinking from a trough that had been sprayed. Homes, automobiles, and even laundry hanging out to dry were spotted with the oily mixture. Birds, fish, and beneficial insects were killed. One man lost 800 colonies of bees. After the disastrous 1957 spraying, the program was drastically cut back. Ironically, the gypsy moth returned. The expensive spraying operation had provided only a temporary solution.

PASSING THROUGH THE FOOD CHAIN

It was once believed that the persistent, or long-lasting, pesticides such as DDT and its chemical relatives were best because they didn't have to be used often. It then became clear that the very fact of their remaining in the environment made them *more* dangerous. Persistent chemicals move up

48

through the food chain, becoming more concentrated with each step up. Although insects may have only tiny amounts of the chemicals in their bodies, birds and small animals eating hundreds of these insects receive large amounts, which they then store in their body fat. As larger birds or animals eat the smaller ones, they receive even stronger doses of the chemicals. Animals and birds further up the food chain, such as eagles and hawks, receive stored chemicals from many food sources. The food chain ends with humans, who may receive the highest concentrations of pesticides.

Persistent pesticides are not metabolized and excreted by the body. They are stored in fat in the tissues of the whole body or in certain organs such as the liver. These chemical residues can accumulate until the organism is contaminated, a process known as *bioaccumulation*. Since only a certain amount of chemicals can be stored in body fat, excess amounts may move into muscle tissue or may affect the central nervous system.

At this point, no one knows exactly what long-term effects the bioaccumulation of pesticides has on humans. Limited studies with volunteers have shown that persistent pesticides at the normal levels found in human tissues are not presently associated with any disease. However, some scientists are concerned that certain agricultural chemicals, alone or in combination, may be linked to certain forms of cancer and difficulties in reproduction and development.

In spite of improved test methods, it is still extremely difficult to detect the amounts of pesticides that individuals or particular groups have been exposed to. Without this information it is difficult, if not impossible, to determine with certainty the effects of chemicals on human health. For the most part, science relies on laboratory experiments with animals and retrospective studies of populations with known chemical exposures, such as groups of chemical workers, to predict human health effects. Although there are many uncertainties in these predictions, this appears to be the best we can do for now.

EFFECTS ON SOIL AND WATER

Soil may look dead and uninteresting, but it is really full of life. In each ounce of soil, up to 2 billion invisible bacteria, fungi, and small green cells called *algae* are breaking down plant residues to release minerals, carbon, and nitrogen into the soil, where they are used by living plants. Some organisms are forming carbon dioxide, which, in some cases, becomes the carbonic acid that dissolves rocks. Microscopic insects are busy breaking down the dead leaves, pine needles, and other plant matter into new soil. Earthworms dig tunnels that aerate the soil, improving its texture so that water can drain through it and plant roots can more easily penetrate it. As the worms eat and excrete organic matter, the soil is enriched. The eighteenth-century English naturalist Charles Darwin showed that earthworms could add a layer of soil 1 to 1½ inches (2.5 to 4 cm) thick in a ten-year period.

All these living creatures depend on the soil, but the soil also depends on them. It is unrealistic to think that the large amounts of insecticide sprayed repeatedly on plants and trees will not eventually make their way into the soil, harming the organisms so plentiful there. This is especially true of persistent pesticides that can build up in the soil. By killing the living matter, pesticides can cause the soil to become hard and fail to hold the moisture needed to promote plant growth.

Some of the chemicals used as pesticides pollute water. Those that are sprayed on lawns and fields can wash into rivers and streams. Chemicals such as atrazine and chlordane have been found in watercourses in the Midwest and other areas of the country. Some chemicals soak through the soil until they come into contact with groundwater—water held in rock formations beneath the earth. Groundwater is the source of drinking water for approximately 50 percent of all Americans.

According to an EPA report, a total of seventy-four pesticides have been detected in the groundwater of thirty-eight states. These come from all sources—agricultural use, spills,

*A variety of pesticides washes into streams and
rivers and can kill large numbers of fish.*

residues from mixing, and so on. Although most of the pesticides found in groundwater have been at levels below established health standards, it should be remembered that the EPA does not yet have complete data on all agricultural chemicals. In addition, it is important to realize that to date the total amount of water testing conducted is relatively small in comparison to the amount of water used for drinking.

EFFECTS ON WILDLIFE

Every year countless birds and animals become sick or die from exposure to pesticides applied to croplands and released into lakes and streams. In addition to those used by farmers, there are other chemicals used by homeowners, golf course operators, and various businesses. These may also directly affect wildlife populations. The pesticides can severely affect reproduction and can eliminate the natural food sources of wildlife. When the USDA sprayed millions of acres in the southeastern states to rid it of fire ants, they received complaints that thousands of quail, wild turkeys, and other game birds had also been killed. Many farm animals either died or gave birth to dead or deformed young.

As a result of studies inspired by Rachel Carson's book *Silent Spring*, the facts concerning DDT's harmful effects on birds and wildlife could no longer be ignored. DDT and similar pesticides were banned in most countries in the 1970s. Some agencies switched to another insecticide, Sevin, which breaks down more quickly than DDT. But although these new pesticides seemed to help the birds, they were extremely toxic to bees. Many beekeepers lost money when their bees were killed by insecticides intended for other pests. Since bees are necessary for pollinating fruit trees, the fruit growers also suffered. In 1970 Sevin killed so many bees in the fruit-growing regions of Oregon and Washington that 2 billion honeybees had to be air-lifted to the area to pollinate the blossoms of fruit trees.

There is another drawback to Sevin and similar pesticides. Although they apparently are not extremely toxic to birds, they are often used during the birds' nesting season and kill many of the insects needed to feed their young.

One of the dangers of the less persistent pesticides is that they have to be applied repeatedly. Although wildlife may be able to recover from a single spraying, it is difficult to survive a continual onslaught of poison. Since the pesticides are often sprayed over very large areas, sometimes thousands or even millions of acres, the wildlife is unable to find a safe haven free of poison.

EFFECTS ON HUMANS

The widespread use of pesticides affects humans as well. Long-term health effects of chronic pesticide exposure include cancers, birth defects, genetic damage, respiratory ailments, liver and kidney damage, neurological disorders, and reproductive problems.

The most serious health problems occur in people who receive heavy exposures of the chemicals during the manufacturing or use of the pesticides. Illnesses caused by chemical poisoning are especially prevalent among farm workers who handle pesticides or work in recently treated fields. An EPA study found that farm workers exposed to organophosphates experienced depression, irritability, and difficulties in thinking, memory, and communication.

How harmful a chemical is to a human depends on the amount that person comes in contact with and the susceptibility of the human to that chemical. Contact with large amounts of pesticides within a short time is believed to be more dangerous than exposure to tiny amounts over a lifetime. The primary hazard appears to be severe short-term reactions to touching or inhaling large amounts of the chemicals.

Accidents and the misuse of pesticides have resulted in a

People heavily exposed to pesticides are often afflicted with serious health problems. Professional exterminators, such as the one pictured here, reduce this exposure by following safety procedures when mixing and using these poisons.

large number of poisonings. The World Health Organization (WHO) estimates that more than 1 million people worldwide are poisoned by pesticides every year, resulting in at least 20,000 deaths. Most of these cases occur in Third World countries, where more use of toxic chemicals is allowed and where they are used without knowledge of their dangers or proper methods of use.

It is not only the active ingredients in pesticides that may cause health problems in humans, but also the inert ingredients such as asbestos, benzene, carbon tetrachloride, chloroform, and formaldehyde. In the process of reviewing 1,200 inert ingredients found in pesticides, the EPA found approximately 50 chemicals that cause adverse health effects, such as cancer, birth defects, and damage to the nervous system. Another 50 have chemical structures similar to those of known toxic substances. The EPA has no information about the potential health effects of some 800 inert ingredients.

At the present time, it appears that although those working closely with pesticides may be at more risk, the small amounts that the general public comes into contact with do not appear to pose a serious health threat. However, this is difficult to determine because of the problems involved in assessing the long-term effects of chemicals in complex ecological systems. It is also difficult to predict accurately the impact of chemical exposure on human health. One of the important lessons we have learned from the history of pesticide use is that determining the full range of environmental and human health hazards from widespread use of chemicals in the environment is not an easy task.

In medicine only a physician can prescribe drugs and medicines. Yet no medical degree is required for a farmer, forester, or anyone else who fills the environment with dangerous chemicals that have the potential for hurting or even killing other people or creatures. It is important that present and future use of pesticides include an understanding of all potential effects on the environment. It is better to suffer a few losses in the battle of the bugs than it is to lose the war against environmental contamination. It is not likely that insects will destroy the world. Nature has provided balances that ensure this won't happen. However, the possibility of man's destroying the world in his attempt to kill what he doesn't like seems much more real and frightening.

PESTICIDES AND
OUR FOOD

The old adage "An apple a day keeps the doctor away" lost some of its clout during the spring of 1989, when many people became suspicious of this popular fruit. Mothers stopped feeding their children apples and poured their apple juice down the drain. Apples disappeared from school cafeteria lunches, and grocery stores noticed an alarming decline in their sale. All this came as a result of a report by the Natural Resources Defense Council (NRDC), a nonprofit environmental group that claimed apples sprayed with the chemical daminozide, sold under the name Alar, posed a risk of cancer in children.

The controversial report by the NRDC, titled "Intolerable Risk: Pesticides in Our Children's Food," claims that the fruits and vegetables preschool children eat may eventually give some of them cancer or neurological (nervous system) problems. The group was especially critical of Alar, a growth regulator used to deepen the red color of apples and to regulate their growth so that they wouldn't drop from the trees too soon. Tests have not found Alar to be carcinogenic, or cancer-causing. However, when Alar breaks down during processing it forms UDMH, a compound that has caused cancer in laboratory mice. This alarming news sent a lot of apples, apple juice, and apple sauce into garbage disposals, even though only 5 to 15 percent of the apples on the market at that time were sprayed with Alar.

The NRDC claims that small children are at greater risk of eventually developing cancer as a result of their exposure to pesticides. This is partly because, relative to their body weight, children consume a higher percentage of fruits and vegetables than do adults. The report claims that this not only exposes them to higher concentrations of pesticides but does so at a time when their immature body systems are less able to remove and excrete the toxic chemicals. Also, exposure to carcinogenic substances early in life allows more time for cancer to develop.

DIFFERING VIEWPOINTS

Although reports such as the NRDC's tend to upset the general public, many of those in the scientific community still have confidence in the safety of our food. One group representing fourteen prominent scientific organizations, and including food scientists, microbiologists, toxicologists, and veterinarians, believes that the public's view of food safety differs considerably from the facts. They feel that the risk posed by such chemicals is slight or nonexistent. Other scientists agree with NRDC's call for better regulation of food chemicals, particularly those that comprise a significant part of children's diets. Others, while urging the public not to panic, also argue for improved regulation.

The EPA also felt that the NRDC report was misleading because of the data used in calculating the risk estimates. These figures, which claim that cancer risks from Alar are

100 times higher than the EPA estimates, were rejected in 1985 by an independent scientific advisory board established by Congress to provide peer review of pesticide actions by the EPA. Another complaint by the EPA was that the food-consumption data used by the NRDC were based on a small survey with only a 65 percent completion rate, whereas the EPA, in a study conducted by the U.S. Department of Agriculture, used a much larger survey of over 30,000 people.

Although the EPA and the NRDC may disagree about the risk estimates, they generally agree on recommendations to improve food safety. This includes the use of more accurate monitoring data on pesticide residues in the food supply and more effective laws for quickly getting pesticides off the market once a problem has been identified.

The controversy over the NRDC study illustrates the fact that the science of estimating human health risks from chemicals is complex and full of uncertainty and disagreement even among respected scientists. Even when the researchers can agree that some health risks exist, there is disagreement regarding what degree of risk should be considered acceptable.

In spite of the general feeling among many scientists that Alar was not an immediate and severe health threat, the EPA banned the chemical in 1989. Many people in agriculture and the chemical business are upset by the banning, not because of the chemical itself but because they feel that largely as a result of public pressure the government acted to ban a chemical previously considered safe. They argue that this opens up the possibility of banning anything simply because of sensational charges made against it while ignoring scientific studies. They caution that regulatory actions should be made on scientific information rather than hysteria. Others feel that the ban on Alar was appropriate and overdue, since the chemical clearly posed some level of risk and since it appears that it was not absolutely essential in the production of apples.

There will probably always be controversies concerning the safety of our food. Although it is possible to see what various chemicals can do to small animals, it is impossible to test humans to determine what levels are toxic. The human body and the environment are resilient and perhaps can handle small amounts of chemicals. Of course, accidental overdoses can have serious consequences. People should not stop eating healthy foods, but our regulatory programs may need to be improved to assure that we keep the amounts of chemical additives in our diets as low as possible.

PESTICIDE RESIDUES

The main fear many people have of pesticides concerns the residues left in or on their food. The types of residues found depend in part on how the pesticide has been applied. Some pesticides are sprayed on the leaves or other parts of the plant that grow above the ground. These pesticides may remain on the surface to prevent the growth of mold, as in the case of fungicides, or may be carried throughout the plant, as some insecticides are. Other pesticides are applied to the soil, where they can be absorbed by the root system and carried to other parts of the plant. When a pesticide residue is found only on the surface of the plant it is referred to as a *topical* residue. Those that are found within the internal tissues of the plant are called *systemic* residue.

Although many of these pesticides may be toxic in their original form, most lose much of this toxicity by the time the plant reaches the consumer. The residue decreases over time; however, some pesticides break down more quickly than others. Some topical residues evaporate or are removed by wind or rain. Even systemic pesticides may break down inside the plant. If the pesticide is applied when the plant is small, its concentration decreases as the plant grows.

Most people think that they can be completely free of

60

pesticide residue if they buy "organically grown" produce. This is not always the case. Although a farmer may not use any pesticides himself, his crops may receive pesticides that drift over from an adjoining field. If persistent pesticides have been used on the field in previous years, the plants may still receive some of the residue through the soil. Also, unless the organic food is strictly regulated, there is an opportunity for unscrupulous farmers to claim falsely that their food is organic in order to sell it at a higher price.

HOW OUR FOOD IS TESTED

Testing to determine the long-term health effects of chemicals is an imprecise science, but an important one. Scientists are able to determine the harmful effects of some chemicals through epidemiological studies—using whole groups of people who have been exposed to the same chemical. For example, by comparing smokers to nonsmokers a strong connection has been made between smoking and an increased incidence of lung cancer and heart disease. Epidemiological studies have also been made of people working in chemical factories. When about half the male workers in a chemical plant in California were found to be sterile, epidemiological studies determined that sterility was caused by their heavy exposure to the pesticide DBCP.

Although epidemiological studies are helpful in some cases, it is much better to determine the harmful effects of certain chemicals before the damage has been done. Since scientists don't want to wait twenty or thirty years to see what effects a certain pesticide may have on a person, they do much of their testing on small animals, mostly rats or mice, with shorter life spans.

Over the years scientists have found that animal testing provides a reliable way to predict which substances will produce cancer in humans. It is assumed that if a chemical induces cancer in a large number of different species of animals, it will also induce cancer in humans. Normally, the small animals used are quite different than humans. But their cellular and molecular structures, where cancer and many other diseases take effect, are similar. These animals have very short life spans, so large doses of the suspected chemical must be administered to speed up the results. Scientists use the results of the animal tests to predict how the drug will affect humans. The most reliable evidence is obtained when several independent tests draw the same conclusion.

There are several different types of toxicity tests conducted on laboratory animals. In the *acute oral* type, the chemical is given to find the dosage that will kill 50 percent of the test animals. The *subacute oral* toxicity test, which is conducted for a shorter amount of time—from three to six months—is done to determine the maximum dose that can be given to an animal without producing any demonstrable effect. At the end of the test period, the animals are killed and their organs examined for abnormalities. *Chronic oral* toxicity tests go on for several generations and are important in detecting the presence of cancer and fetal deformities.

Animal testing can be very time-consuming and expensive. New tests that allow scientists to test more chemicals in less time have been developed. Perhaps the most promising is the Ames test developed by Dr. Bruce Ames, a professor of biochemistry at the University of California at Berkeley. In this test, food substances are placed on sterilized plates with about a billion *Salmonella* bacteria. Samples of the chemical to be tested are placed on some of the plates, while others are left as controls. The bacteria can grow only under the test conditions if some of them mutate, or change their genetic material, in order to make an important missing nutrient. After two days, if the plates containing the chemical contain more colonies of bacteria than the control plates, it means that the chemical caused mutations in the bacteria. Since substances that cause mutations may also cause genetic birth

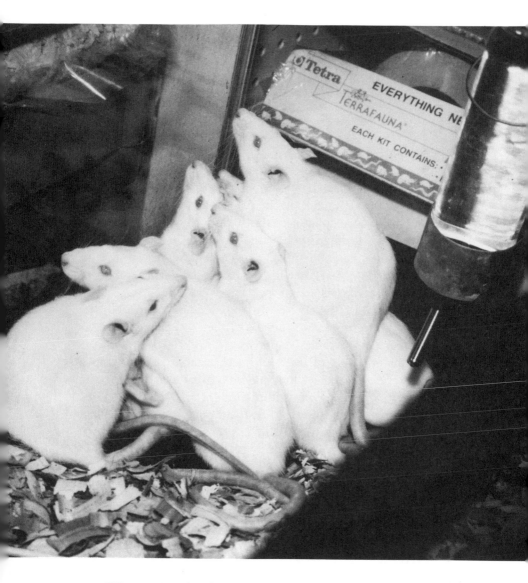

*When testing for the potentially harmful effects of
the chemicals used in pesticides, scientists often do
their research on small animals, such as these rats,
which have much shorter life spans than humans.*

defects and possibly cancer, the findings of the test are significant. With the Ames test, scientists can detect mutagens and potential carcinogens in just three days and at considerably less cost than that of other types of tests.

WHO TESTS OUR FOOD?

In order to protect America's food supply, various federal and state programs have been set up to monitor levels of pesticide residues in our food. Testing is also done by the chemical companies developing new pesticides. In the United States most of the testing is conducted by the EPA, the Food and Drug Administration (FDA), and the U.S. Department of Agriculture (USDA). In addition to these agencies, others in at least thirty states test for pesticides on food.

The EPA is authorized to register pesticide products, specify the terms and conditions of their use prior to marketing, and remove unreasonable hazardous pesticides from the marketplace. Part of their job is to establish the tolerance level for any pesticides that may leave residues in food. The *tolerance level* is the maximum amount of residue presumed not to present a health risk. Tests are required to determine, among other things, the pesticide's potential to cause chronic illness, reproductive disorders, birth defects, and cancer, as well as environmental damage. For pesticides now being developed, the producer must present data showing the product's effects on health and the environment. The EPA uses the data to evaluate the pesticide, balancing its benefits against its risks.

Once the EPA sets tolerance levels for the various pesticides, it is up to the FDA to see that these restrictions are observed. The FDA is responsible for monitoring food shipped interstate, whether it is grown domestically or imported from other countries. The FDA collects domestic food samples as close as possible to the place where they were produced. If they find a food that may be harmful, they have the authority to remove it from the market. If the food is imported, the FDA can detain shipments at their port of entry.

The FDA also conducts the Market Basket Study, also known as the Total Diet Study. This ongoing study attempts to estimate how much total pesticide is consumed by males and females in eight different age groups, ranging from infants to the elderly. Staffers from the FDA purchase 234 individual food items from common retail outlets in three different cities, cities that change each year. Seasonal purchases are made four times yearly. The selections are based on nationwide dietary surveys. The foods are prepared as they would be in the average home and are then analyzed for pesticide residues and other substances. Since pesticide levels are usually lowered during preparation by washing, peeling, and cooking, this testing method most closely determines the actual amounts of pesticides being consumed.

The Market Basket Study and other tests analyze foods for residues from some 253 pesticides. This includes many commonly used pesticides but not all of those presently in use. The FDA assumes that the residue levels of the untested pesticides are similar to those tested.

The USDA monitors pesticides in the meat and poultry they inspect. They work with the FDA under the Food Safety Inspection Service (FSIS). This group notifies the FDA whenever an inspection turns up an illegal amount of pesticide or other chemical, including drugs such as hormones used in animals, in the meat or poultry being inspected.

PROBLEMS OF FOOD TESTING

In spite of testing by various agencies and pesticide manufacturers, it is still impossible to say with certainty that all our food is absolutely safe. It is presently impossible to analyze all types of foods for all pesticides. There are an enormous number of pesticide/food combinations that need to be tested. In many cases, testing is made more difficult because of a lack of information on what pesticides actually have been used on certain crops. Also, the mechanisms used for testing pesticide residues are not sophisticated enough to detect all the residues that may be present. The FDA concentrates on the pesticide/food combinations thought to have the greatest potential health risk to the consumer.

When it comes to testing, all pesticides are not created equal. According to the Delaney Clause, a 1958 amendment to the Food and Drug Act, no chemical that has been shown to cause cancer in animals can be added to processed food. This means that pesticides found in processed foods must follow stricter regulations than those in foods that are not processed. To make matters more confusing, pesticides registered before 1978 follow different restrictions than do those that have come up for review more recently. The EPA currently requires pesticide manufacturers to submit as many as 150 tests on the environmental and health effects of pesticides. But most pesticides used today were registered either before modern testing requirements were in place or before the EPA existed.

Another testing problem concerns foods imported from other countries. Many countries, especially in the Third World, do not regulate pesticides as strongly as the United States. Imported food products may contain not only more pesticides than domestically grown produce, but also pesticides banned for use in our country. By this process, often called the "circle of poison," pesticides banned at home return to consumers through the residues on some of the food they import. Many people feel that if these products are too toxic to be used in our country, they are too toxic to be used anywhere. They want industrialized countries to prohibit the export of pesticides that have been banned, canceled, severely restricted, or never registered in our own country.

The FDA has improved its ability to monitor imported foods, especially fresh produce. In 1986 the agency purchased the Battelle World Agrochemical Data Bank, a computerized data base containing information on worldwide pesticide use. This helps the FDA know which pesticides are most likely to be used on which imported foods. The agency can require certification from all shippers from a country where illegal residues are commonly tolerated. Since the certification can take time, it automatically detains the foods not meeting our standards.

Food testing appears to be working. Agencies at both the federal and state levels are looking longer and harder for pesticides on foods and are finding less. During 1988 the FDA, in its Tolerance Enforcement Program, sampled almost 18,000 food samples (7,600 domestic, 10,000 imported) for the presence of 200 different pesticides. Less than 1 percent of domestic samples was in violation, along with about 3 percent of imported samples.

REDUCING THE RISKS

A careful distinction must be made between levels of pesticide residues found on raw, untrimmed, unwashed, unprocessed food and food that is actually eaten. Most food processing and preparation do away with a substantial amount of pesticide residue. Organophosphates, which are not commonly found as residues in food, are usually transformed into harmless compounds during cooking. There are some exceptions. For example, when daminozide (Alar) breaks down during processing it forms UDMH, a compound that has caused cancer in laboratory mice. But in most cases, processing adds an extra level of protection against pesticide residues.

There are ways in which consumers can cut back even further on the amounts of pesticide residues. Pesticides

67

stored in fat can be largely avoided by trimming away fat on meats and by using low-fat dairy products.

Any pesticide residues on the outer layer of produce can be eliminated by washing all fresh fruits and vegetables in running water. The produce can also be washed in a mild detergent as long as all the residue is rinsed off. Removing the outer layer may also be helpful. Wax coatings found on cucumbers, peppers, and some apple varieties, for example, may contain pesticides and may also hold in the pesticides that have been sprayed on the produce's skin.

Consumers who want to ensure that no pesticides have been used during the growing process can buy organically grown produce. This type of produce may be harder to find and may cost a little more, but as the demand increases, so should the supply. Many consumers prefer to grow their own fruits and vegetables as a way of controlling the pesticide residues on their food.

Even if consumers don't buy organically grown produce, they should at least choose carefully and make an effort to buy only domestically grown produce and in season. Produce imported from other nations may contain residues of pesticides banned in the United States. Consumers also should not insist on perfect-looking produce since it takes more pesticides to attain this perfection.

With so much controversy over the safety of our foods, it may seem as if it is dangerous to eat anything. This is not true. The single greatest cause of cancer is cigarette smoking, which accounts for nearly a third of the cancer deaths in the United States. The rest are caused by a wide variety of other factors, including heredity, environmental causes, and foods. Even where foods are concerned, cancer specialists consider our high-fat, low-fiber diet to be more of a factor in the development of cancer than pesticide residues. In fact, not eating fresh fruits and vegetables, many of which are believed to contain certain vitamins and enzymes that may slow down or even help prevent cancer, is more likely to increase cancer risks than are the traces of pesticide residues that may be found on those foods. This does not mean that we should ignore the potential health risks associated with pesticide residues, just that we should keep them in perspective. As in all things, common sense goes a long way toward living a healthy life.

BIOLOGICAL CONTROL

In the late 1800s, many California citrus growers faced economic disaster. Their trees stopped growing normally, and the fruit the trees produced was deformed. The cause of the damage was some innocent-looking patches of white fuzz, which were actually egg masses containing thousands of eggs of the cottony cushion scale. The scale insects fed on the trees' juices and caused their stunted growth and deformed fruit.

By 1880 the menacing cottony cushion scale had spread throughout California and had damaged thousands of citrus trees. Finally, in 1888, the citrus growers sent an entomologist, or insect expert, to Australia to find a natural enemy to the scale. Albert Koebele brought back some Vedalia beetles (ladybugs) and a type of parasitic fly. As soon as these new insects were released into the citrus orchards, they began to reproduce and soon spread throughout citrus-growing areas. By the end of the project's first year, the scale population had been dramatically reduced.

The idea of using insects to control other insects was not a modern one. Hundreds of years ago, Chinese citrus growers used predatory ants to control certain pests attacking their citrus crops. Growers in the Orient still maintain or purchase colonies of predatory ants to reduce the numbers of leaf-feeding insects on their orange trees.

BIOLOGICAL CONTROL

Using natural enemies to control pests is referred to as *biological control*. The natural world is very organized. For every plant, animal, or insect on earth there is some natural enemy that will keep its population in check. Weather conditions, such as temperature ranges and rainfall, limit the area in which certain pest species can live. Mountain ranges, deserts, large bodies of water, and other geographic barriers also keep pests in their place.

Nature was able to keep things fairly well balanced until humans started changing things. They moved plants, as well as insects, across countries and even across oceans. They got rid of the variety of plants in the fields and replaced them with monocultures, setting themselves up for unmanageable infestations of insects that preferred those crops. But whereas working against nature has created pest problems, working with nature can help to control them.

Biological control uses natural predators, parasites, or diseases to control the population of a pest species. It has been referred to as the "thinking person's pest control." Those who favor pesticides try to control pests by using a product. Biological control experts try to solve the same problems by using a process.

Natural enemies for pests include predators, parasites, and pathogens. Predators are animals or insects that kill other animals or insects for food. Parasites are organisms that live on other organisms referred to as their hosts. Pathogens are substances or organisms that cause disease. Some 200 insects and a half-dozen weeds have been brought under control by these various natural enemies.

PREDATORS

Insect predators capture and eat large numbers of insects. Some of these tiny meat eaters even have tough sounding names, such as the ant lion, dragonfly, tiger beetle, and pirate bug. Most predators are large compared to their host (prey). Some lie in wait to pounce on their prey; others chase their victims down in order to eat them. If the prey is not able to move around much, the predator can simply graze on the host population.

Some predators have chewing mouthparts that allow them to chew up their victims. Others have piercing mouthparts that suck out the juices, and the life, from their victims. These predators often inject a powerful toxin that paralyzes their prey and prevents the unlucky victim from thrashing about. The larvae of predators must consume several insects in order to stay alive, which often makes them even more helpful than the adult form in combatting pest insects. For example, the larva of a single ladybug may consume hundreds of aphids before it is developed. Most predators feed on the same kind of host during both their immature and adult stages.

The best predators have an appetite only for a specific insect. (Some predators, such as the praying mantis, are good at eating large numbers of insects, but they eat the good ones as well as the pests.) Helpful predators also need the ability to search for their prey. If they blunder around the garden they may not be able to find enough of the pests to keep down the population. Effective predators should also be able to increase in number along with the pest and should be able to live in a wide range of environmental conditions.

Ladybugs or lady beetles are effective predators against aphids, scale insects, and other plant-eating insects. A single ladybug may eat hundreds of aphids to get the energy she needs to produce a batch of eggs. For this reason many farmers or fruit growers release large numbers of lady beetles into their area to feed on the aphids and scales on their crops. The only disadvantage to ladybugs is that they often fly away as soon as they are released.

Not all insect predators are other insects. Toads, lizards, frogs, moles, and shrews are just some of the many forms of wildlife that exist on a diet of bugs. Some birds eat their own weight in insects every day. Since these birds tend to eat the most prevalent insects, they are especially helpful in controlling outbreaks of pests.

At night the American toad comes out of hiding to search for cutworms, potato beetles, chinch bugs, ants, slugs, and a number of other small creatures. The toads have few enemies because their skin is covered with a foul-tasting slime. If the weather is moderate, these toads can stay active for seven or eight months each year. In that time a single toad can eat up to 15,000 insects.

Some people choose pets to take care of their insect problems. One popular creature is a gecko, a type of lizard. The gecko likes roaches and can deroach a house in two weeks. Unfortunately, once the roaches are gone, the owner must find other insects, such as crickets, for their gecko's dinner.

Natural enemies can also be found for some weeds. The most successful example of this is the Klamath weed. In the early 1900s it was found in northern California near the Klamath River, from which it got its name. The Klamath weed spread rapidly across the dry western United States and soon became a serious pest for ranchers. It not only crowded out valuable forage being grown for livestock but also produced weight loss and sores on the animals. The weed also caused financial losses because of lower land values and poorer quality cattle. Although some chemicals could combat the spreading weed, using them was much too expensive. The weed covered too large an area, much of it inaccessible.

By 1944 the Klamath weed had taken over about 5 million acres of rangeland in five states. That year, some natural enemies of the Klamath weed were brought from Europe, including three species of beetles and a gall midge. Once entomologists were sure that the beetles would rather starve to death than eat the valuable crops in the area, they released them. The results were even better than most enthusiasts had expected. A ten-year survey completed in 1959 showed that 99 percent of the weed had been eliminated. The remaining 1 percent was needed to maintain a population of beetles as protection against a future increase of the weed.

PARASITES

Parasites are creatures that live off other creatures. The word comes from the ancient Greek word *parasitos*, meaning "feeding beside," or "one who eats at the table of another." The word was first used insultingly to refer to people who ate at another's expense. Perhaps this is why the insect being eaten is politely referred to as a "host."

Parasites don't kill their host outright, but use the host as a source of food for nurturing their young. Some parasites deposit eggs within the larvae or eggs of their prey so that their own developing young can feed on the host. Others use a sticky solution to attach their eggs to a caterpillar, the common name for larvae. When the eggs hatch, the parasite larvae bore through the skin of the caterpillar to reach a supply of food. Still other parasites merely lay their eggs on a leaf where an unsuspecting caterpillar will eat them. In all cases, death comes slowly for the host as the hatching larvae usually avoid feeding on its vital organs until near the end of their development.

Most female wasps deposit their eggs in or near the particular food that the young will eat. Here, a parasitic wasp lays her eggs in a tobacco budworm.

Although some parasites feed on a number of different hosts, many are host-specific, meaning that they attack only a single species. This trait makes them more effective than predators in controlling a specific pest problem. But unlike predators, which eat large numbers of insects in their lifetime, a parasite usually eats only a single animal. By the time the host dies, the young parasites are usually mature enough to mate and lay their own eggs.

PATHOGENS

Pathogens, or microbes, are animals or plants that produce substances that injure the host. The pathogens most often used in pest control are bacteria, viruses, fungi, and protozoa. These pathogens may kill the insects, affect their ability to reproduce and develop, or make them more vulnerable to other insects, diseases, or human-made controls.

One advantage to using pathogens is that different diseases affect different insect species. This allows pest control experts to make a certain pest species sick while not bothering the beneficial insects in the area. Another advantage is the fact that although insects may develop a resistance to chemical controls, it is believed that they do not develop a resistance to diseases.

Bacteria: Although most of these tiny one-celled organisms are beneficial, some cause diseases. One bacterial disease used in pest control is the milky spore disease. It has been successful in killing the larvae of the Japanese beetle, which feeds on the leaves and fruit of trees. By 1953, federal and state governments had worked together to spread the disease through fourteen eastern states. The disease greatly reduced the population of the Japanese beetle and has kept it low except for small local outbreaks. One advantage to bacterial diseases is that once the land is treated with bacteria, it remains in the soil for years.

By far the most successful bacterial insecticide used

commercially is *Bacillus thuringiensis*, referred to simply as Bt. A naturally occurring bacterium that can be produced artificially, Bt produces crystals so toxic that the hosts die within a week. Commercial production of this pathogen began in 1958, and today Bt is used against a wide variety of pests in fields, forests, and gardens.

Viruses: Another form of pathogen used in controlling insects is the virus. Although viruses have the advantages of being highly host-specific and presumably safe, they are hard to mass-produce economically. Since viruses can live only within living cells, they can be produced only from live, infected insects. At one time these host insects could be raised only on their host plants. Now some of the insects thrive on artificial food, so it is easier and cheaper to raise them year round.

A viral insecticide has recently been developed to control bollworms and budworms on cotton and other crops. It has been estimated by researchers that if this insecticide were used on all U.S. cotton acreage, it could replace more than a million pounds of chemical insecticides. However, cotton growers have been slow to accept the new virus as an insecticide because it takes three to six days for the disease to kill the bollworm, whereas chemical insecticides kill them within a matter of hours.

Much research still needs to be done to develop economical and safe ways to use viruses in pest control. For example, some viruses are harmed by ultraviolet light, and ways need to be found to get them onto crops while protecting them from sunlight. Viruses also need to last longer on crops and to spread farther and faster on their own.

The EPA is testing viruses for their safety. The biologists who developed them feel that viruses are safe because they already exist in nature. Nearly everyone has unknowingly consumed an assortment of viruses in food without any apparent harm. However, people haven't consumed viruses in the amounts that might be present if these pathogens become

*Overcome by a viral insecticide, a
cotton bollworm hangs from the boll
of a viral-protected cotton plant.
At the slightest touch, the caterpillar
will rupture, and release billions of
additional virus particles that could
spread to protect other plants as well.*

more widely used on food crops. At this point, no one knows for sure whether there would be any harmful effects of these extra viruses on human health. To combat this possible problem, scientists are altering viruses genetically so that they will be short-lived and will pose no threat of uncontrolled spreading. In a 1989 experiment a genetically altered virus of this type was released in a cabbage patch. It killed all the cabbage loopers as it was supposed to, then died before it could harm anything else.

Fungi: Entomologists feel that naturally occurring fungi are very important in keeping insect populations under control. Although only a few are available commercially, more are being developed. One type of mold is already in limited commercial production. When applied to the roots of seedling pines and other cone-bearing trees, the molds protect the trees against disease and speed up the process of getting water and nutrients from the soil to the roots. Studies have shown that treated seedlings can grow twice as fast as untreated ones.

Other experimental molds guard cotton, soybeans, potatoes, and many other important crops against the wilt known as "damping off," and may save onions, beans, and lettuce from the white molds that make them shrivel and die. These molds are not produced commercially yet because the market is too small, but this may change as the cost of pesticides rises.

An Australian fungus is having success in killing grasshoppers. The fungus produces enzymes capable of penetrating a grasshopper's tough outer skeleton. It then circulates in the insect's blood, attacking body tissues and fat reserves. The grasshopper dies within a week but the fungus lives on, producing spores that spread in the environment and attack other grasshoppers in the area. It does not harm other insects. Once U.S. scientists confirm the safety of the fungus, they hope to infect batches of grasshoppers in laboratories, then release them into crop areas plagued by the pests.

USING BIOLOGICAL CONTROLS

The success of using natural enemies against the cottony cushion scale in California in the 1890s prompted more attempts at controlling pests with introduced predators and parasites. This method was seen by many entomologists as being a permanent, simple, and inexpensive way to handle other agricultural pest problems. However, many natural enemies have provided disappointing results. Some imported predators do not adapt to their new surroundings. For example, a species of beetles was brought from Australia to be used as a natural enemy of mealybugs in California. The beetles were effective in getting rid of large numbers of mealybugs but were not hardy enough to survive California winters. This led to the practice of raising insects in insectaries, then releasing them in large numbers in infested groves each spring and summer. This technique, called *periodic colonization,* was first used in 1919 and continues to be used today.

Finding the right natural enemies for pests is a complicated procedure. Once entomologists determine a plant's origin, which is no easy task in itself, they must often depend on the cooperation of like-minded scientists and governments around the world. After the natural enemies have been found, brought back, and tested for safety, they are cleared for release. But getting them established in the automated and artificial setting of today's agricultural world is not always easy. They are often hindered by pesticides, ongoing disturbances of the area by agricultural operations, and removal of noncrop vegetation that might otherwise provide them with food and shelter.

Once insects are introduced into nature, it is impossible to remove them. There is concern that bringing foreign insects into the country might backfire, and that the new insects might become pests themselves. To prevent this, experts take special precautions to see that no harmful insect

Before being released in the United
States, biocontrol insects, such as
the flea beetles USDA entomologist
Gaetano Campobasso is watching, are
caged with as many as sixty-five
different crops and ornamental plants to
ensure that they eat only the target weeds.

pests, plant pathogens, or parasites are released. The USDA requires all imported insects, plants, or plant parts to be quarantined in insect-proof laboratories until they are thoroughly tested. Before releasing any insects for biological control, scientists want to ensure that the natural enemies are bound so closely to the pest species that they will not bother other beneficial insects or plants.

Extensive testing is especially vital before releasing natural enemies of weeds. There can't be the slightest chance that plant-eating insects will develop a liking for crops of economic value. For instance, it would be terrible to bring in an insect to get rid of thistles and later discover that it also liked to eat corn. Fortunately, many insects are quite host-specific and are adapted to living on just one or a few kinds of foods.

ADVANTAGES AND DISADVANTAGES OF BIOLOGICAL CONTROL

In the long run, using biological control methods is less expensive than using chemical pesticides. This is due in part to the rising cost of pesticides that results from the increased expenses involved in producing and testing today's complex pesticides. Not only are chemical pesticides often expensive, they must be used continually, especially since they kill the natural enemies of the pests they are trying to control. The pests keep returning, often in greater numbers than before. But once biological control is established, it costs little or nothing to maintain from year to year. The natural enemies normally continue to reproduce and to remain effective as long as pesticides are not used to eliminate them. Even when biological control alone is not completely successful, it may decrease the amount of chemical pesticides needed.

Unfortunately, biological control is not always as simple as it sounds. Although hundreds of predators and parasites have been shipped to the United States from several countries in hopes that they would control pests, many were unsuccessful. Some could not survive the trip or life in their new environment. Others, who did survive, could not reduce the numbers of the pests they were brought to control. And some parasites and predators did not reproduce enough or at the right time to reduce pests effectively.

Biological control takes a great deal of knowledge of the pests themselves, of the natural enemies available to control them, and of the surroundings of both. Much of the success in biological control depends on exact timing. Experts must study the life cycle of the pest to find its most vulnerable stage, which determines the most effective time for natural enemies to be released.

Some growers are not interested in biological controls because they do not provide the "quick fix" that chemical pesticides offer. Unfortunately, reverting to chemical solutions can destroy all the work done in the area of biological control. In California, after the Vedalia beetles successfully controlled the cottony cushion scale, some citrus growers again began spraying poisons to kill aphids. The poison also killed the Vedalia beetles and parasitic flies, and the cottony cushion scale became a serious pest again.

Biological controls are not preferred by growers who do not want to see any bugs at all. These methods do not eliminate a pest species completely. They reduce the population only enough to keep the damage minimal.

At the present time it is difficult, if not impossible, for biological control to replace the use of chemical pesticides completely. Yet predators, parasites, and pathogens could help save at least some of the 30 percent of U.S. crops each year that are damaged by pests and could help our country lessen its dependence on chemical pesticides.

OTHER ALTERNATIVES
TO PESTICIDES

When people think of the arsenal of weapons available against pests, they rarely think of everyday items such as window screens, freezers, vacuum cleaners, flyswatters, or even a heavy foot. Yet these are just a few of the alternatives to pesticides in fighting the battle of the bugs. On a larger scale, farmers can reduce pest problems by altering some of their farming methods. Many of these changes involve choosing what to plant, when or how to plant it, and what to do after the crops have been harvested.

PHYSICAL AND MECHANICAL CONTROLS

Physical and mechanical controls are perhaps the simplest alternative to chemical pesticides. Some have been used for thousands of years. Even people in ancient times used smoke to keep flying insects away and various forms of flyswatters to get rid of the ones that came too close.

Some physical methods use barriers, things as simple as

putting screens on the windows to keep out flying insects or building a fence around a garden to keep out rabbits and other hungry wildlife. Barriers can also be used to catch insects. Bands of sticky material can be placed around tree trunks and the stems of large plants to prevent crawling insects from doing damage. Flying insects can often be caught on a sticky surface such as flypaper. Wood ashes scattered around the base of plants discourages many crawling or walking insects.

Some insects, especially those in stored products, can be controlled with heat or cold. Weevils, tiny insects that can get into cereals, flour, and other dry products, can be eliminated when the food is put in the freezer for a while or heated in the oven. Not many pests can survive in temperatures higher than 120 degrees F (49° C). One researcher used heat to get rid of termites. He blew hot air into houses wrapped in tarpaulins to raise the temperature, even in the centers of large wooden beams, to 120° F (49° C). After thirty minutes, all the insects were dead.

Other physical and mechanical methods can be used to remove pests or to prevent them from multiplying. Mosquito populations can be reduced by draining off standing water or coating it with a thin layer of oil to stop the female mosquito from laying eggs there. Many pests can simply be washed off plants with a heavy spray from the garden hose. Pet owners who frequently vacuum their homes help keep flea populations down by removing the eggs that have been laid in carpeting, furniture, and their pet's bedding. Some giant vacuums are even being used experimentally in fields. One vineyard uses a large vacuum cleaner mounted on a grape harvesting machine to suck insects off the plants, then spit them out as mulch. Because of their expense, these vacuums may never become widely used, but they have allowed some California strawberry and lettuce growers to cut pesticide use by more than 40 percent.

Traps are another common method of getting rid of unwanted insects. Most of them work by exploiting an insect's need for food, shelter, or sex. Traps for roaches and ants are sold commercially for use in homes and businesses. Even a simple thing like a cabbage leaf turned upside down acts as a trap for snails, slugs, cutworms, and other pests that come out at night to eat plants. Lights can attract insects to be trapped or electrocuted in "bug zappers," although these devices may also kill beneficial insects.

Weeds are controlled mechanically by pulling, digging, or cultivating. This gives instant results because the weeds can be removed from the site so that the area looks better immediately. Unfortunately, these methods require a lot of time and hard work, especially for large areas. Also, if the weeds are removed when they have ripe seeds, the seeds are spread over a wider area. However, this is still the best alternative to herbicides.

On a larger scale, quarantine is an important element in pest control. In 1912 Congress enacted the Plant Quarantine Act to regulate the movement of living plants from state to state and from country to country. Many states have inspectors at their borders to ensure that no agricultural products are brought in illegally. Plants coming into the United States from another country must also go through quarantine measures.

CULTURAL CONTROLS

Cultural controls involve changing the environment or farming methods in a way that will discourage pests. Before pesticides became plentiful, most farmers relied on cultural controls to reduce the number of pests damaging their crops. Many of these practices fell by the wayside during the glory days of pesticides. But now that pesticides have become so expensive and are recognized as potentially harmful, many farmers are coming back to these controls.

One of the most effective cultural controls is *crop rotation*, or the planting of a series of different crops. This method, which has been practiced by farmers since ancient times, not only improves soil fertility but prevents the buildup of a pest population that feeds on one kind of plant. If a farmer keeps planting nothing but corn, the insects that feed on corn will stay with the crop because they have a steady source of food. But if something else is planted, such as soybeans, rye, or clover, this breaks the insect's cycle because other types of insects feed on these plants.

Severe outbreaks of a single pest can also be eliminated through *mixed cropping*. This simply means planting a variety of crops in an area instead of a monoculture. The more area covered by a monoculture, the more attractive it will be to that crop's enemies. One reason for this is that insects find their food through chemicals produced by their host plant. In a monoculture, this signal is much greater. Also, with so much food available, the insect doesn't have to look very far for the next meal.

Planting a mixture of crops encourages a mixture of bugs, some of which will be beneficial and will thereby reduce the chances that a particular plant eater will overrun the crops. Some cotton growers plant strips of alfalfa between strips of cotton. This draws one damaging pest away from the cotton, where it can do serious damage, into the alfalfa, where it is not as harmful.

Similar to mixed cropping is *companion planting*, in which certain plants are mixed in with the primary plants to help in pest control. Some of the companion plants provide food and housing for the natural enemies of the primary plants. For example, wine growers found that planting blackberries near their vineyards increased the number of tiny parasitic wasps that attacked the grape leafhoppers damaging the grape crops. These plantings are often referred to as *trap crops*. Trap crops are made up of plants that are even more desirable to pests than the primary crop. Once the pests are lured into the trap crops, they can be killed with pesticides or some other means of pest destruction.

Other companion plants actually ward off certain insects. Garlic, marigolds, and mints are known for their built-in repulsiveness to bugs. Marigolds excrete a chemical into the soil that keeps down the nematode population in the immediate area. And garlic is offensive to almost all pests. These repellent plants give some protection to neighboring plants within a distance of about 3 feet (0.9 m).

Some plants, such as the sundew, pitcher plant, and Venus flytrap, turn the tables and eat the insects instead of letting the insects eat them. These plants trap insects with their leafy parts and digest them in a fluid secretion.

Some cultural controls are based merely on timing. Insects usually make their appearance at the same time every year, so farmers may be able to plan their planting to ensure that crops grow when pests are not as numerous or active. For instance, when cotton is planted late, it is more likely to be damaged by the boll weevil because the cotton will reach maturity at a time when the weevil population is large.

Plowing at the right time may destroy a particular life stage of a pest. Plowing in the fall or early spring can expose grasshopper eggs to freezing or drying or can bury them too deep for the nymphs to reach the surface after hatching.

Another cultural control involves *sanitation*, or cleaning up waste vegetation to discourage pest infestations. Sanitation involves destroying or plowing under the dead plants after harvest to get rid of the pests that would spend the winter in the plant residues. Burying stalks, weeds, and other residues after harvest destroys eggs, pupae, or hibernating larvae and adults. Practicing good sanitation can also help prevent certain diseases. Many microorganisms spend the winter in debris, ready to attack the young and vulnerable plants in the spring. By getting rid of the debris, these organisms don't have a chance to strike.

Texas agriculturists realized the value of destroying cotton stalks after harvesting. A Texas law, passed in 1987, requires cotton growers to shred cotton stalks and plow them under about three weeks after harvest. This process destroys the food sources and protective homes of the damaging boll weevils. Modern technology helps enforce this law. Using infrared photographs taken from airplanes or from the French satellite *SPOT-1*, scientists from the Agricultural Research Service are able to identify harvested fields in the Rio Grande Valley in which the stalks have not been plowed under. Scientists estimate that plowing the cotton fields after harvesting will cut in half the number of times the fields will need to be sprayed with insecticides the following year.

Another method of cultural control is *strip harvesting*. This is used only with field crops, such as alfalfa, which provide several cuttings of hay in the same season. Instead of harvesting an entire field at once, farmers may choose to harvest a crop in alternate strips at different times. When an alfalfa field is cut all at once, all the insects, including the beneficial ones, either die or move out of the area. By harvesting the fields in strips, the natural enemies can move from the cut areas into the strips where alfalfa still stands. When pests begin to attack the new growth, the pests' enemies are already there to stop them. This method allows farmers to spend less on spraying, but it isn't always the most economical use of harvest crews and equipment.

RESISTANT VARIETIES

Most people think of plants as defenseless against insects and disease, but they do have ways of fighting back. The plants that do well at fighting off certain insects and diseases are called *resistant*. They either repel pests or grow well in spite of them.

Through aerial infrared photography, USDA entomologist Ken Summy easily identifies unplowed or regrowth cotton that should be destroyed to control overwintering boll weevils.

There are different types of resistant plants. *Non-preference plants* either contain something that repels a pest, or simply lack the stimuli that would make the plant interesting to the pest. Some plants have colors that certain insects don't like. Others have bad odors or tastes to make them unappealing or lack certain odors that attract egg-laying insects. Some plants have fuzzy leaves or sharp spines that are uncomfortable for certain pests. Other plants are so tough that insects can't chew through them.

Antibiotic plants contain materials that can either kill an insect, affect its ability to reproduce or grow normally, or make it too sick to eat much. These plants may contain certain oils that repel insects or fungi. Some plants seem to produce these oils only when they are under attack; others, such as garlic and marigolds, always have a good supply. Some antibiotic plants produce *antifeedants*, chemicals that eliminate an insect's appetite before it eats enough to harm the plant. Insects who lose their appetite do not grow properly and are more susceptible to diseases and predators.

The third type of resistance that plants may experience is *tolerance*—the plants can just sit there and take it. The plants do not actively try to kill or damage the pests but are able to regenerate their damaged tissue rapidly enough to stay healthy in spite of attacks. It appears that these plants can produce more growth hormone to replace damaged leaves or root systems. Not only can they heal their wounds, they can also resist any diseases that may enter the affected area.

Plant breeders work continually to produce new resistant varieties. Normally, they isolate plants and expose them to a particular insect or disease. They use the hardiest survivors to breed new plants. As a result, each generation of the plant is more resistant than the last. It takes several years to develop a resistant strain, and unfortunately, this resistance doesn't always last. Plants that become resistant to one type of insect may become more susceptible to another. And some insects build up their own resistance to the plant and can once again become serious pests.

92

Plant breeders monitor the pests and diseases affecting plants. When a new pest or disease surfaces, breeders begin developing a new strain of plant that will be resistant to the new threat. It usually takes several years for the new pest or disease to multiply to the point of being a serious problem. By that time plant breeders will probably have produced a new resistant variety.

Resistant varieties are not perfect—there is no way to develop a plant resistant to all pests. And there is often a trade-off involved. Plants bred to be resistant may lose something in taste, nutritional quality, or some other characteristic. Also, some of the resistant varieties produce toxic natural insecticides. These are not believed to pose any real health hazard, but plant breeders must ensure that in their quest for insect-free plants they do not make food less healthy.

INTERFERING WITH REPRODUCTION

One obvious way to cut down on the number of insect pests is to cause them to stop reproducing at such phenomenal rates. Scientists have been experimenting with ways to interfere with the insects' ability to reproduce. One area of experimentation deals with *pheromones*, the natural perfumes, or attractants, that many insects give off to attract mates of their species. These attractants are necessary to guarantee that the insects will find each other during their brief mating season.

So far, pheromones for nearly 700 insect pests have been identified. Scientists have been able to duplicate some of these in laboratories and use them in a variety of ways. The most common use of pheromones today is in baiting traps. Some of these traps lure pests to their death. The traps can be laced with pesticides or pathogens, depending on whether captured insects are to be killed directly or released to infect others.

Traps are most often used to count various kinds of insects—to determine what pests are in the area or to moni-

*A good catch of lesser peach tree
borers is inspected by USDA technicians
Kathy Scarborough and John Blythe as
they check traps that have been baited
with small amounts of pheromones.*

tor the movement of certain insects spreading into new areas. For example, entomologists in Texas are using traps baited with bee-attracting pheromones to track the movement of African bees, often referred to as "killer bees," as they move from Mexico into Texas.

Pheromones may be used to lure pests away from valued crops and to concentrate them in small areas where they can be more easily killed by pesticides or beneficial insects. They can also be added to insecticides to increase their effectiveness by luring pests into the treated areas.

Pheromones are sometimes used to confuse insects. When the scent is spread over a wide area, the males have difficulty in finding females to mate with. Since their life spans are short, many die before they can mate.

At first pheromones were used only with insects considered to be pests. Now scientists see the advantages of using pheromones to attract beneficial insects to prey on the pests. Pheromones can lure beneficial insects into an area to start new colonies or can draw them away from a field about to be sprayed with insecticide. The first patented pheromone for a beneficial insect was for the spined soldier bug, an excellent predator. A single soldier bug can eat up to fifty eggs a day of such pests as the tomato hornworm and the Mexican bean beetle.

It makes more economic sense to produce pheromones for beneficial insects than for pests. Each species of insect responds only to a specific chemical, which limits the market for any one pheromone. Since beneficial insects often eat a number of pest species, one pheromone could be used to control several different pests. For example, the spined soldier bug is known to eat over a hundred different pests, so a pheromone for this insect would have wide market appeal.

As with all other methods of pest control, the use of pheromones has its limitations. Pheromones are attractive only to the adult stage of the pest, yet it is the juvenile forms, such as caterpillars, that do most of the damage.

Another way scientists can interfere with an insect's

reproductive function is through the *sterile-insect control method*. In this method insects that have been made sterile, or unable to reproduce, are allowed to mate with normal insects of their species but no offspring are produced.

Edward F. Knipling, who worked for the USDA, first used this method successfully to eliminate the screwworm flies harming livestock throughout the southern states. Knipling found that exposing the screwworms to X rays sterilized them without affecting the way they ate, flew, or mated. When these sterilized flies were released, they mated with normal flies, but no offspring were produced. Knipling theorized that if this were done for several generations, eventually the screwworm fly population would be reduced to nothing.

Knipling's theory proved successful in eliminating the screwworm flies on Sanibel Island off the coast of Florida and on the island of Curaçao in the Caribbean Sea. But his biggest test came in 1958 when he was asked to eliminate screwworm flies from more than 50,000 square miles (129,500 sq km) in Florida and nearby states. For eighteen months, a "fly factory" set up in an airplane hangar produced 50 million flies a week. Twenty airplanes spread the flies over Florida and parts of Georgia and Alabama. By early 1959 the screwworm fly was eradicated, although as insurance more flies were released during the next year. The male-sterilization technique is often successful, but it is not permanent. Sterile screwworm flies are still released on a regular basis to act as a buffer zone between the United States and Mexico, keeping the flies out of our country.

A new technique uses a lower dose of irradiation, which does not leave the male sterile but causes him to produce sterile offspring. Scientists mate the irradiated males with normal laboratory females and harvest the eggs to store and distribute in infested areas. The larvae hatching from these eggs mature and mate normally, but their sterility causes a drop in the population of the next generation. There are many advantages to working with eggs instead of adult insects.

96

*Entomologist Frank Herard watches a
wisp of smoke in a laboratory wind
tunnel that helps him track the movement
of insect pheromones in the air.*

Eggs are less fragile than adults, are easier to handle and transport, and can be stored for months, increasing production capacity by as much as a thousand times.

Sterility methods do not work with all insects. In some species the radiation does more than make an insect sterile. It may change some other characteristics such as ability to mate. The technique is expensive and is best suited to insects present in comparatively small numbers.

HORMONES

All living systems, including plants and insects, have chemical communication systems called hormones; the hormones cause the systems to mature on time. In insects, these hormones regulate their passage through the various stages to adulthood. Exposing insects to specific hormones during certain stages can disrupt these timetables. The insects may pass through stages at the wrong time or may never reach adulthood.

There are two kinds of hormones of interest to entomologists—*juvenile* hormones and *molting* hormones. Juvenile hormones are needed to make immature worms grow larger, but the hormones must disappear before the

Eggs that will produce sterile gypsy moth larvae are being inspected by entomologist John Tanner. The eggs are harvested and kept in cold storage. The larvae hatching from these eggs mature and mate normally, but their sterility causes a drop in the population of the next generation of gypsy moths.

99

worms can become sexually mature adults. The molting hormones control the rate at which the insects shed their outer covering in order to grow. Both of the hormones are necessary for the normal growth and successive molting of immature insects. When the insect reaches the end of its larval or nymphal stage, the flow of juvenile hormones decreases and the insect becomes a pupa, and eventually an adult.

A larva treated with a juvenile hormone will continue to molt and grow larger, but it will never become an adult capable of reproduction. If juvenile hormones are given to adult females during their reproductive cycle they affect the insect's ability to lay eggs. When the insects are given molting hormones, their development is accelerated and they die prematurely.

From the standpoint of reducing the amount of damage done by certain insects, the use of hormones is not very effective. The treated insects may not lay eggs, but they continue to feed and can do a lot of damage before they die. Some newer products combine hormones with insecticide. Any insects not killed by the insecticide are unable to reproduce and cannot pass on their resistance to later generations.

Some plants contain natural hormones that kill insects or prevent them from maturing. For example, balsam firs contain a chemical that causes the nymphs of the linden bugs to secrete so much juvenile hormone that they can never mature. Other balsam trees produce chemicals that affect the development of other groups of insects. As a result, balsam trees are relatively free of pests.

Scientists are now experimenting with chemical insecticides that affect the hormonal systems of insects. One insecticide, chlordimeform, interferes with a particular hormone and causes the insect to change its behavior. Researchers found that just a few bites of a leaf sprayed with chlordimeform caused caterpillars to become so disoriented that they left the plant. When an insect's eggs were treated with this chemical, the larva stopped feeding; this resulted in

100

unsuccessful hatching. The second chemical, methoprene, mimics the juvenile hormone. When insects were exposed to methoprene at the wrong stage, they became sterile adults.

Using hormones to control pests has many advantages. They appear to affect only the insects and have not been found to be toxic to humans and other vertebrates. Many are quite host-specific and thus do not harm beneficial insects. And most of these growth-regulating chemicals degrade rapidly, not lasting long enough to harm anything else.

Alternate means of pest control are limited only by man's ingenuity. Some of them, such as electronic insect repellers, appear not to work. Others, such as hormones for insects and rotation of crops, may become commonplace in the near future. Whatever the alternate methods are, they are important in finding more economical and environmentally sound practices of pest control.

INTEGRATED PEST
MANAGEMENT

A total reliance on pesticides to control pests is a no-win strategy. Pests come back in even greater numbers, or build up a resistance to the pesticides being used. And insects that had never caused much trouble before often become serious pests when their natural enemies are eradicated. Also, the costs of pesticides are skyrocketing to the point where many farmers cannot afford to use them in such large quantities. Finally, people are becoming more concerned with the effects of the pesticides on their food, their health, and their environment. Clearly, there must be a better way.

Some growers are opposed to the use of any type of synthetic chemicals, including fertilizers, pesticides, growth regulators, and feed additives. Farming without using any of these chemicals is referred to as *organic* farming.

Organic farming requires a wider knowledge of plants and insects than does farming with chemicals. Organic farmers rely on more of the old-fashioned methods of fertilizing their crops and keeping insects under control. Among other things, they use crop rotation, animal manures, off-farm organic wastes, and mineral-bearing rocks to feed nutrients to the soil. Weeds are controlled through cultural methods such as crop rotation, as well as with hoes or mechanical cultivators instead of herbicides. Insects are controlled through various biological methods. When pesticides are used, they are normally natural compounds such as natural bacteria and insecticidal soaps.

There are many misconceptions about organic farming. Some people think it is a step backward to inefficient, old-fashioned methods. Although it is true that organic farming does use many of the methods relied on by early farmers, it also uses modern technology. Most of today's organic farmers use modern farm machinery and up-to-date knowledge of crop varieties, livestock management, and soil and water conservation practices. To keep insect populations to tolerable levels, they use biological, mechanical, and cultural controls.

Other people believe that although organic farming may work for the backyard gardener, it is not practical for large commercial farms. However, there are approximately 30,000 commercial farmers reported as using no chemicals to any great extent. A five-year study by the Center for the Biology of Natural Systems at Washington University in St. Louis, Missouri, has shown that some midwestern corn farmers have implemented organic farming practices and still make money in the competitive farm economy of the corn belt.

Others think that organic farming is too costly because the yields on organic farms are generally lower. In most cases the money lost through lower yields is offset by the money saved by not using expensive chemicals.

In spite of the advantages of organic farming it is not often possible to carry it out in its purest sense, especially in large-scale operations. But although a total absence of chemicals may not be the answer, neither is the present practice of dumping tons of harmful chemicals on our earth year after year. The best solution is integrated pest management (IPM), also referred to as alternative agriculture; it uses the best of both systems.

IPM relies less on blanket spraying of chemicals and more on a sophisticated understanding of both plants and pests. This system combines several control methods, including biological controls, chemicals, resistant plants, cultural controls, and a variety of other alternatives. The goal of IPM is not to annihilate pests totally, but to reduce their numbers to levels that are not damaging to the economy. It tries to achieve the maximum amount of good with the minimum amount of harm to the environment.

Many of the alternatives used by IPM are the same as those used in organic farming—rotating crops, planting a variety of resistant crops, and using natural enemies to keep pests under control. Chemical pesticides are limited to specific problems and are usually used in smaller amounts. IPM seeks to minimize the disadvantages in the use of pesticides and to maximize the advantages. A report compiled by the Congressional Office of Technology Assessment in 1986 estimated that IPM techniques could cut pesticide use by as much as one-half.

USING INTEGRATED PEST MANAGEMENT

IPM is a more sophisticated approach to farming than is traditional chemical farming. Instead of using a calendar to dictate when crops should be sprayed with chemicals, farmers using IPM study their own situation to determine when treatment is needed, where it is needed, and what strategy to use. These strategies may involve physical, cultural, biological, or chemical controls or, more likely, a combination. The best methods are those that are the least disruptive to the natural controls already in place. For example, when growers use chemicals to kill a wide range of insects, they also kill the natural enemies of the pest. As a result, they inherit the job of killing the insects that would have been killed by natural enemies. With IPM, farmers take advantage of the natural enemies already in place.

An IPM program includes a monitoring system to determine when some action must be taken. This requires an awareness of what pests are in the area, which of their natural enemies are available to take care of them, and even what environmental conditions, such as the weather, could affect the pest problem.

Pest monitoring often makes use of traps baited with pheromones or some other attractant such as light. These traps are useful in timing pesticide applications so that they are used only when enough pests are present to cause significant damage. Farmers can also time the emergence of adult insects so that insecticides can be used more effectively during the pest's brief egg-laying stage.

Once growers know what pests are in the area, they must determine how much damage those pests are likely to do. The presence of some pests doesn't necessarily mean that they will cause economic loss. In fact, having some pests may be helpful because it maintains the population of predators, parasites, and pathogens. An insecticide that kills 50 percent of the pest insect and none of its predators may be more valuable than one that kills 95 percent of all the pests, including natural enemies.

Sometimes even large numbers of pests can be present without affecting the yield or quality of the crop enough to make spraying worthwhile. However, when enough of the pest species are present to cause real damage, the cost of control is justified. This is known as the *economic injury level* for that crop and pest, the point at which the cost of controlling the pest is less than the cost of the potential damage it can do.

Instead of widespread spraying, people using the integrated pest-management system spray only the areas being affected by pests.

Once the grower determines that the pest problem is serious enough to require action, what strategy to use must be determined. At this point, some type of pesticide may be necessary. But even when chemicals are used in an integrated program, careful attention is paid to the timing and the amount used to get the most effective control with the least harm to the environment. For example, insecticides are sprayed only on the small areas affected by the pests, rather than blanketing the entire area with poison. It is also more likely in IPM that the pesticides used will target a specific pest instead of being broad-spectrum pesticides that may also kill beneficial insects.

The methods used to apply the pesticides may also cut down on the amount needed. It has been shown that less than 20 percent of the insecticides broadcast as dusts and less than 50 percent of those sprayed actually reach the plant surfaces for insect control. In all, only about 1 percent reaches the target insect. By improving the methods of applying the insecticide, less is spread needlessly into the environment. Better application methods include using low-volume spraying rather than high-volume spraying. Treating seeds, especially with systemic insecticides, requires very little pesticide and can be very selective in the insects affected.

When possible, IPM also involves attracting more natural predators and parasites to control the pests. In forests it may mean planting nectar-bearing plant species among the trees to attract parasites and predators to kill pest insects. In the future, pheromones will probably be used more often to lure beneficial insects into an area.

IPM VERSUS CHEMICAL CONTROL

Chemical pesticides are no longer the cheap and effective way to wage war on bugs. In the 1950s and 1960s, when pesticides such as DDT could be used with a clear conscience, they cost about 20 cents a pound. Today, the chemi-

*USDA entomologist Nacanor Liquido
places fruit fly traps in a papaya
grove in order to monitor
the fruit fly population.*

cal pesticides are more difficult to make and require so many safety tests that the cost has skyrocketed to as much as $400 a pound for some chemicals. In spite of higher costs, many insects fail to respond to the newer, more expensive chemicals. In 1935 it was estimated that seven insect species were resistant to pesticides. Now nearly 500 species are resistant to at least one pesticide, and some species are resistant to all of them. In addition to insect pests, some 70 types of weeds are now resistant to herbicides.

Integrated pest management is also more beneficial to the environment. Farming with this method works with nature rather than working against it. Fewer dangerous chemicals are fed into the environment to cause problems later on. And since fewer chemicals are used, there is less likelihood that insects will build up a resistance to the pest-control methods. This will extend the lifetime of the insecticides now available. The reduced need for pesticides has the added bonus of reducing the number of potentially dangerous chemical factories. It also reduces the need for storage and disposal sites, which can often be a problem, especially in crowded cities.

The environment is not the only thing to gain. IPM can save farmers money. The profits in agriculture are not great enough to withstand the high costs of pesticides. A survey taken in California showed that pest control was the largest cost for citrus growers in parts of Ventura County in 1980. The growers spent about $375 per acre to buy and apply chemical pesticides. That was more than they paid for irrigation, fertilization, weed control, pruning, frost protection, and other day-to-day needs. Two years later, after various natural enemies had been introduced, the growers were able to cut back on their use of pesticides. Their pest control costs dropped to $160 an acre.

The savings may not always be so great. Some of the potential savings in pesticide costs may be offset by the additional technical training needed for IPM. Another expense may be the need for people to spend more time in the field, monitoring insect populations and evaluating different techniques. But spending money on expert advice instead of on chemicals is a good trade-off.

The main disadvantage of IPM is that it is more difficult to carry out. IPM requires both a knowledge of the environment and more decisions. However, there are now computer programs that can help. These computer models can, with some success, predict whether or not a pest will reach a threatening level. Predictions are made by combining daily weather data, field sampling, and advanced computer technology that simulates actual conditions. The computer models also take into account the value of the crop and the cost of the control measures to determine the economic injury level.

Some computer models are also able to predict diseases for plants. Once these programs are perfected, accurate forecasting techniques will result in better disease control and a reduced need for pesticides. Forecasts have already been developed for more than two dozen major diseases, and scientists are working on two dozen more. The models consider the type of plant, the disease and environmental factors, especially moisture and temperature, and the way they all affect the pathogen. Although application of computer simulation models is still fairly new, these models have an increasingly important role in loss predictions. The goal is to create estimates far enough in advance so that growers can adjust their plans.

ROADBLOCKS TO IPM

In spite of the fact that integrated pest management is less costly and much safer than the present chemical war on pests, it is still not used as much as traditional chemical methods. There does not seem to be enough scientific evidence to

111

convince growers to change to safer methods. There are too many roadblocks in the way, many involving economic factors.

Agriculture is a big business governed by the profit motive as much as any other. Many growers are reluctant to try IPM because they are afraid of what will happen if IPM doesn't work. Their livelihood depends on raising high-quality, high-yield crops. One bad year could mean economic disaster. They feel they can't afford to take chances. And since IPM is a more complicated system requiring the cooperation of experts from many different fields of study, many farmers do not feel qualified to try it. It is much easier to continue doing what they have been doing for years, that is, spraying chemicals as insurance that pests will not be a problem.

In most cases, switching to IPM would have to be a gradual process. It takes time for the insects in fields, forests, and orchards to return to a natural state. Farmers switching from conventional methods to IPM could suffer short-term losses while they learn the new techniques. In order to make the switch to IPM, farmers need expert advice and inexpensive sources of parasites, predators, and pest pathogens. Guaranteed government assistance could help ease the financial uncertainties of transition.

The multibillion-dollar pesticide industry has even more to lose if IPM becomes popular. It provides jobs for thousands of people, from the researchers who develop and test the product, to the factory workers who produce the chemicals, to the salesmen who promote the product, to the people who apply the pesticides. The industry's primary interest is in developing profitable pesticides and promoting their use, not in encouraging people to cut back. Some chemical companies, however, recognize that there may be a promising future in providing farmers with information on crop varieties, pest cycles, weather conditions, and other important factors affecting pest control and other services associated with IPM.

Economics also plays a part in determining the types of pesticides being produced by chemical companies. From an environmental standpoint, the best pesticides are selective ones that kill pests but leave beneficial insects alone. These pesticides would ultimately cost the grower less and would be less damaging to the environment. However, it is not profitable for chemical companies to make pesticides with such a limited market. They can make more money with broad-spectrum pesticides that effectively kill many different kinds of pests and therefore appeal to a lot of different people.

In fairness to the chemical companies, it must be noted that developing new pesticides has become an extremely expensive business. Forty years ago, simple pesticides such as DDT could be synthesized in only one step. But producing the newer pyrethroid pesticides, considered to be much safer, requires thirteen separate steps and much more elaborate production facilities. Added to this are the millions of dollars needed to conduct the numerous tests required for having a pesticide registered by the EPA. According to the entomologist Robert Metcalf in the article "Changing Role of Insecticides in Crop Production," in 1956 an estimated $1.2 million was the cost of developing a new pesticide. By 1984 that cost had risen to $45 million. Chemical companies also face huge liabilities if their chemicals cause unexpected damage.

Before being too critical of the pesticide industry, it must be remembered that it is unrealistic to expect any company, chemical or otherwise, to spend more putting a product out than they could ever hope to earn from it. The development of biological control methods means that there will be less of a payoff for an individual chemical company. Biological controls are often targeted to a small number of pest species and thus have less of a future sales market than would wider-spectrum chemical controls. Also, retaining the sole rights to the use of a biological control method may prove difficult, although a company may clearly hold a patent on a particular chemical formulation.

But although the pesticide industry's profit motives may be understandable, their influence over our pest control methods may not be. Farmers get much of their advice from pesticide salesmen, and many of these salesmen recommend spraying schedules based on the calendar instead of need. This is referred to as "preventive treatment" or "insurance" spraying. Most farmers are also led to believe that the only good bug is a dead bug. Naturally, this attitude insists on a heavier use of pesticides than does a belief that a few insects won't matter much. Since salesmen are motivated to make a sale, many farmers receive poor advice and may use too much pesticide, use it at the wrong time, or use it when it isn't even needed. This encourages return business, as customers need more chemicals every year.

Another major roadblock to IPM is the difficulty involved in making the transition from traditional chemical farming. In many cases, integrated control or alternative farming is most effective when applied to large areas. In some cases, programs of biological control may be jeopardized by landowners who decide not to cooperate and spray their own property with pesticides. However, many benefits of alternative farming systems may be realized on a single farm operation.

Forcing people to use IPM raises the question of individual rights in pesticide use. On the one hand, growers should have the right to spray their fields with chemicals if they want to. However, if their use of chemicals is harmful to others or to the environment, they should not have that right. For example, pesticides may drift onto the property of those who do not want them. Excessive use of pesticides by some farmers may also kill some of the beneficial insects needed by neighbors or may hasten the development of pests resistant to a particular pesticide. The new pesticide-resistant species of pest will bother not only the farmer who used the chemicals excessively but also others in the area and will leave neighbors with no means of combatting the pests.

If IPM is to be widely adopted, pesticide users must be

made aware of their options and must receive proper training and information on successful and appropriate IPM programs. First, county extension agents and others who advise farmers on their pest control problems need to be convinced of the value of IPM. It is only through access to sound information that farmers can learn enough about IPM to implement it. Instead of using pesticide salesmen to diagnose problems and recommend their treatment, pest control advice should come from specialists in IPM. The number of these specialists is growing, but there are still too few to make the needed impact.

Second, more research money needs to go to the development of safer pest control strategies. It is unlikely that the chemical companies will pay for such research because it will hurt their business. Therefore, farmers, government agencies, and universities must be involved in the research.

Since farmers are taking the biggest risks in switching from their present pesticide practices to IPM, Congress should modify farm support programs to reward growers for using fewer chemicals. For example, instead of giving farmers financial benefits through subsidies for growing only one or two specialized crops, the government should reward them for using a more varied rotation. Another benefit the government could provide would be insurance against any losses caused by the new procedures. Farmers would then not be so afraid to take the risks involved in making the changes.

Last, as a nation we need to change our attitudes about our methods of agriculture. Chemical pesticides have been the mainstay of agriculture for so many years that it is difficult to envision another way of doing things. Changing current practices would require a change in national policy. Using alternative methods may take more people, but even this has some advantages. With so many unemployed, would it provide needed employment to have more jobs on farms?

In most cases, IPM offers a commonsense compromise between those who are totally dependent on chemicals for pest control and those who want no chemicals used. In untouched areas, the balance of nature may be sufficient. But our agricultural practices have created an artificial imbalance, one that favors the survival of plants over that of insects. Man created this imbalance and now, for economic reasons, must struggle to maintain it. Although a total ban on all insecticides is unrealistic, it is also unrealistic to think that total pest control can result from use of chemicals alone. Integrated pest management can get farmers off the "pesticide treadmill" and on to a more reliable and economical form of pest control.

LOOKING AHEAD

The subject of pesticides is one of concern to a wide range of people, all with conflicting interests. The pesticide industry is interested in the profits it can make from the sales of its products. The agricultural community is interested in how it can produce the highest yields for the least amount of money, something that is made more difficult by the high costs of pesticides. Environmentalists are concerned with the hazardous effects chemical pesticides have on the environment. And in the middle of everything is the government, criticized by both the pesticide industry and agriculturists for saddling them with too many regulations, and by environmentalists for not doing enough to enforce those regulations. It is easy to see that there is no way to keep everyone happy.

No matter how these various groups feel about pesticides, it is clear that they are here to stay. In spite of the problems caused by today's heavy use, other problems would surface if all pesticides were suddenly to disappear. Pests destroy much of the food we grow that is needed to feed a rapidly expanding world population. Pests also threaten human lives with the diseases they carry. For these reasons, pesticides are presently a necessary part of our world. The problem is not with pesticides themselves or even with chemical control. The problem is in using chemical control as our *only* strategy in pest control.

CAUSES OF PESTICIDE OVERUSE

Today's pesticides came about as a result of human ingenuity, but their overuse is a result of human limitations. Chemists are able to devise new combinations of chemicals to get rid of pests, but these chemicals have been used without a full understanding of how they affect our finely balanced ecosystems. We must remember that every time a chemical is used for anything there will be both benefits and risks associated with that use. History shows that we often don't know for many years what those risks will be.

Chemical solutions appeal to a society that craves quick, easy answers to every problem. We still hold out hope for instant miracle cures for everything from colds to cancer to obesity. This same attitude causes us to look for the fastest way to get rid of bugs, weeds, or anything else we consider ugly, damaging, or inconvenient. The agrichemical industry uses this attitude to develop advertisements that play to our desire for a "quick fix."

In his book *Biological Control by Natural Enemies*, Paul DeBach, professor of biological control at the University of California, refers to pesticides as "ecological narcotics" and compares the exclusive use of chemical pesticides to the use of addictive narcotics. In each case, instant results are seen. But before long, the amounts and frequency of use must be increased as a tolerance, or resistance, to the chemicals develops. This eventually results in a habit that is difficult to break. In both cases the realization emerges that the actions were unwise, but withdrawal is a slow, difficult, and painful process. It takes a long time to get a human or an ecosystem back to normal after these kinds of abuses.

The desire to make a profit has also played a significant role in the overuse of pesticides. The popularity of DDT made chemical companies realize that there was money to be made in pesticides. Since then, billions of dollars have been spent, not only in producing new pesticides but in promoting them as the only means of pest control.

Even the federal government is partly to blame for pesticide overuse by failing to investigate all of the harmful effects on the environment. Government agencies now review certain tests on new pesticides before they can be marketed, but the EPA, the testing agency, is so far behind that harmful chemicals are allowed to stay in use until further studies can be made.

CUTTING BACK ON PESTICIDE USE

It seems an impossible task to overhaul our present system of pesticide abuse to reach a sensible level of pesticide use. The most difficult job will be to change attitudes, those of the growers who provide our agricultural products and of the consumers who demand that these products be perfect. Growers will have to learn that the mere presence of an insect pest is not a cause for alarm. But growers will not be able to relax their stringent use of pesticides until buyers are willing to accept blemished produce. Almost one-quarter of all pesticides are used to destroy pests that affect only the appearance of produce.

Persuading consumers to buy less-than-perfect produce will not be easy. Years of advertisements have encouraged us to expect spotless food. Changing this attitude will require a massive public education campaign. In addition to changing attitudes, government grading standards will have to be relaxed so that produce will not have to be flawless to be marketable. Taking such action is not without risk. Consumers might buy fewer fruits and vegetables if they weren't as attractive, and this would result in economic damage for farmers.

If attitudes could be changed, society could force legislation to demand safe and selective pesticides, in turn forcing the chemical industry to provide safer alternatives. These pesticides might be more expensive, but that would further encourage more sparing use. In many cases, higher prices have already encouraged some growers to look more seriously at integrated pest control practices in order to reduce their operating expenses.

LOOKING TO THE FUTURE

Biotechnology: As in most areas of science, the future holds the potential for remarkable advances in the field of pest control. One of the most important areas of study will be in the field of biotechnology, sometimes referred to as genetic engineering. In biotechnology, scientists manipulate the genetic systems of bacteria, viruses, plant cells, animal cells, and so on to produce an organism that might never emerge in nature. For example, scientists are able to transfer a gene for a desirable trait from one species to another. Biotechnology is used in many areas of science, including medicine and agriculture.

Today, scientists not only can alter existing genes but can construct totally synthetic genes to cause an organism to perform desired functions. More research is being conducted to show that genetically engineered bacteria living inside crop plants can churn out desirable chemicals such as insect and fungus deterrents and growth-enhancing nutrients. Laboratory tests have shown some success in using genetically altered bacteria to protect corn from the European corn borer. However, some of these same tests have shown lower yields.

Each year hordes of European corn borers, eating as much as 10,000 times their weight each month, destroy $400 million worth of crops in the United States. One company has used genetic engineering to develop a product that tackles this pest. It uses a type of bacterium called an *endophyte*, a common organism that can live harmlessly inside a plant. Spliced onto the endophyte is a single gene from the Bt bacterium, which is deadly to the corn borer. Pressurized containers force the new bacteria through the tiny cracks appearing naturally in corn seeds. As the corn plants grow, the new bacteria multiply in the sap, killing European corn borers feeding on the stalks. The bacteria stay in the stalks and do not migrate into the kernels or seeds. It is estimated that 30 million pounds (13.6 million kg) of chemical insecticides are used annually in the United States to fight the corn borer. Because only a small number of microbes would be needed to treat seeds, and because they reproduce within the plant, it is estimated that 30 pounds (13.6 kg) of genetically engineered microbes could be used to treat the entire U.S. corn crop.

Another important area of genetic engineering is development of plants that are more resistant to diseases. Because disease resistance is controlled by a relatively few genes, this area is one of the most favorable candidates for early application of biotechnology to plants. However, it is possible that insects and disease organisms will adapt to these genetically altered plants just as they did to chemical pesticides.

Genetic engineering may also be used more to develop highly specific insect pathogens to produce insect disease or affect the insects' immune system, thus making them more vulnerable to other diseases. It may even be possible to change insects genetically in a way that would interfere with their normal growth or maturation. However, our knowledge of how genetic alterations will affect insect behavior and insect ecology is still very rudimentary. But some methods of biological control have the potential to benefit from genetic engineering and improve the effectiveness of natural ene-

121

mies. Since these processes are highly specific to single insect species, they may prove to be good alternatives to chemical pesticides.

Biotechnology may someday enable plants to give off pheromones for certain insects. Scientists have found several unique enzymes in insects' pheromone glands. These enzymes are produced by genes that eventually can be identified and possibly inserted into plant material. The plant itself can then be a slow-release source of pheromone for disruption mating or for attracting beneficial insects.

Although there are many opportunities for using biotechnology, there are also many potential problems. For example, work is presently being done to make crops and forest trees that are resistant to herbicides. Although these new crops might ease the work load of the farmer by allowing him to spray his weeds away instead of using more time-consuming methods, they also encourage an increased use of herbicides. This could potentially increase the risk of contamination to the environment, groundwater, foodstuffs, and farmworkers exposed to the herbicides.

Perhaps the major concern about the field of biotechnology is that too little is known about it to be able to judge its risks accurately. In the past, we have embraced new technologies only to discover later that they had some consequences we didn't anticipate. Although absolute safety cannot be guaranteed, certain regulations have been enacted to reduce the risks. Biotechnology companies are regulated by the Environmental Protection Agency, the Department of Agriculture, the Food and Drug Administration, and the Occupational Safety and Health Administration. Among other things, these federal regulations require that genetically altered organisms must be evaluated for safety before being tested outdoors. Scientists conduct extensive tests in laboratories and greenhouses to ensure that the organisms are not toxic to humans, animals, or beneficial plants or insects.

Electronic technology: Computers are an important part of almost every field today, and pest control is no excep-

*Instead of producing pheromones
to lure pests, scientists are
now experimenting with pheromones
to lure parasites and predators,
such as the spined soldier bug,
to areas where they are more
likely to find pests to feed upon.*

tion. One of the most important ways computers can help is by giving easy access to up-to-date information. Several computerized data bases provide results of the latest research, reports, and articles that might help people needing advice on controlling pests. One data base uses the research done by the Agricultural Research Services (ARS). The ARS staff in Beltsville, Maryland, reviews ARS research reports and chooses the ones thought to be of value to extension education programs. The ones considered most practical and applicable are placed in the Extension Service Electronic Information Network for electronic retrieval.

Today's computers can even do much of the thinking for humans, through a capacity called *artificial intelligence.* The most practical application of artificial intelligence is an expert system, or a computer program designed to reason like a human expert in some field. For example, in integrated pest management, mathematical models can help in determining the best course of action to take with a pest control problem.

Computer models are only as good as the science that goes into them. Good models require thorough research into the crop plant itself and the organisms that affect it, such as insects, diseases, and weeds. When good computer models are established, they have some obvious benefits. Their greatest benefit to IPM is that they can make short-term predictions on the pest population trends, crop yields, or quality of a particular crop. Long-term predictions are less accurate because crops and their pests are both affected a great deal by weather factors that are impossible to predict correctly over a long period of time. The models can also

In the future, computers will be used even more extensively as data banks for pesticide information, and to make short-term predictions on pest population trends and crop yields.

provide extremely valuable insight into the injury potential of certain pests.

Biological control: Much research will concentrate on increasing the use of natural enemies over a wider range of pest species. This will involve research here and abroad to match up various species of natural enemies with hosts. Research may also find ways of mass-producing natural enemies, possibly through the use of artificial diets. This will ensure that the "good" bugs outnumber the "bad" bugs. Genetic engineering may also be used to produce more effective natural enemies, such as those with more acute sensory organs or other beneficial traits that give them an advantage over the pest species.

Scientists may also find ways of manipulating habitats to make them more attractive to natural enemies. This has already been done to some extent by irrigating to change a habitat or by introducing other plants into a monoculture in order to provide food and shelter for natural enemies. And researchers are looking for ways to help natural enemies locate their hosts more quickly. There are already experiments with pheromones to lure parasites and predators to areas in which they are more likely to find pests. Until recently, most of this research centered around finding pheromones for pest insects, so there is much to be done to develop pheromones for beneficial species.

More research is also being done on the use of hormones. Manufacturers of urban pesticides, such as ant, roach, and flea killers, have already begun to include these hormones in some of their pesticides. These are often advertised as "birth control" for pests. So far, using hormones in pesticides is impractical on a large scale because in an open environment it is difficult to get the substance to the pests at the right stage of their development. Part of the problem is that hormones break down easily and are thus not available to the insect at the right time. More research is needed before this method becomes practical.

Research scientists are also developing ways to manipulate chemical signals to trick insects. Scientists at Cornell University have discovered that aphids, when seized by a natural enemy, emit a warning chemical that sends other aphids fleeing from the plant. When the scientists sprayed plants with a synthesized form of this alarm chemical, they found that other aphids would not return to the area. But again, there is still a great deal of work to be done in manipulating such chemicals for practical use.

Chemical pesticides: Researchers hope to develop more selective chemical insecticides that would not be as damaging to a pest's natural enemies. Pesticides that are safer for the environment are also being researched. The recent introduction of insecticidal soaps shows promise in controlling many soft-bodied insects, including aphids, mealybugs, whiteflies, and some scale insects. Unlike household cleaning agents, which can injure plants and animals, biodegradable insecticidal soaps penetrate insects' membranes and burst cells, yet spare beneficial honeybees, ladybugs, and wildlife. When researchers mixed soaps with smaller amounts of pesticides, they found that the soaps not only controlled pests but also acted as adhesives, keeping the pesticide mixture on the plant longer.

The trends in pesticide use appear to be toward a "less is best" attitude. The newer pesticides will be equally effective at lower dosages. They will also be more specific, controlling one pest while not affecting beneficial insects. There will also be new application techniques, such as vaccinating seeds, which will cut down on the amount of pesticide that drifts where it is not wanted.

If pests are judged by the amount of damage they do to our environment, then the world's most dangerous pests are humans. It was through human ingenuity that pesticides were first developed. Human carelessness allowed these chemicals to threaten the environment. Now it is time for human ingenuity to come up with ways for pest control measures and the environment to work together. We must accept the fact that we will never gain control over insects. As a wise scientist has said, "The object of our game with nature is not to win, but to keep on playing."

GLOSSARY

Antibiotic plants—Plants that produce chemicals that can kill, sicken, or affect the reproduction or growth of insects.

Biological control—The control of pests through the use of their natural enemies—parasites, predators, and pathogens.

Botanicals—Pesticides derived from plants.

Chlorinated hydrocarbons—A class of chemical compounds, such as DDT, that are produced by the addition of chlorine atoms to hydrocarbons.

Cultural control—The control of pests through the use of farming methods or any methods that change the physical environment so that the damage caused by pests is reduced.

Defoliation—The premature loss of leaves from trees or plants.

Entomologist—A scientist who studies insects.

Fumigant—A poisonous gas used to kill insects in enclosures.

Fungus—Any member of a group of very simple plants that contain no green coloring matter (chlorophyll), including molds, mildews, mushrooms, and bacteria.

Fungicide—A chemical that kills a fungus, a common cause of many plant diseases.

Herbicide—A chemical that kills plants and is used to control weeds.

Hormone—A product of living cells that circulates in body fluids or sap and produces a specific effect on the activities of other cells.

Insecticide—A chemical or biological agent that kills an insect.

Integrated pest management—The control of pests by a combination of methods such as chemicals, natural enemies, resistant plants, and cultural and mechanical controls.

Larva—The wingless, often wormlike form in which insects hatch from their eggs.

Metamorphosis—A change in physical form, structure, or substance, such as the change of a caterpillar into a moth or butterfly.

Molt—To cast off periodically an outer covering that is then replaced by new growth.

Monoculture—The cultivation or growth of a single crop in an area to the exclusion of all others.

Nematocides—Poisons used to kill nematodes, the tiny worms that harm many plants and agricultural products.

Organophosphates—A class of insecticides containing phosphorus that works by disrupting the nerve function in insects.

Parasite—A plant or animal living in or on another organism.

Pathogen—Any agent that causes disease, including bacteria, viruses, and fungi.

Persistent pesticides—Pesticides that remain in the environment and do not degrade, or break down, into a harmless form for months or even years.

Pesticide—Any agent that kills an animal or plant unwanted by man.

Pheromone—A chemical substance produced by an adult insect when it is ready to mate, which attracts adults of the opposite sex.

Predator—An animal, insect, or other organism that kills other animals, insects, or organisms for food.

Pupa—The stage in an insect's complete metamorphosis when it is enclosed in a cocoon or pupal case and emerges as an adult.

Residue—The amount of a substance, such as a pesticide, that remains on or in an agricultural product.

Resistance—The opposition offered by a plant or animal to disease, poison, or other threat to its survival.

Resurgence—The return of a pest species to an area that had previously been cleared of that pest through the use of pesticides.

Rodenticide—A poison used to control rodents such as rats, mice, or gophers.

Saprophytic fungi—Fungi that feed on dead plant and animal matter.

Secondary pests—Insect species, formerly considered harmless, which become pests after pesticides kill off their natural enemies.

Systemic—A pesticide that enters the circulatory system of the plant or animal rather than attacking only the surface.

Topical—An application of a pesticide to the surface of the plant or animal. Also, a pesticide residue that is found only in the outermost surface of a food.

SOURCES

Blockstein, David E. "Pesticides Remain a Problem for Congress." *BioScience*. April 1988, p. 231.

Bohmont, Bert L. *The New Pesticide User's Guide*. Reston, VA: Reston Publishing Co. 1983.

Budiansky, Stephen. "Farmers to Pesticides: Bug Off." *U.S. News & World Report*. October 13, 1986, p. 69.

Carson, Rachel. *Silent Spring*. Boston: Houghton Mifflin. 1962.

Crowley, John, Ed. *Research For Tomorrow*. Washington, DC: U.S. Department of Agriculture. 1986.

Debach, Paul. *Biological Control by Natural Enemies*. London: Cambridge University Press. 1974.

Dethier, V. G. *Man's Plague*. Princeton, NJ: Darwin Press. 1976.

Fichter, George S. *Insect Pests*. New York: Golden Press. 1966.

Garland, Anne Witte. *For Our Kids' Sake*. New York: National Resources Defense Council. 1989.

Gay, Kathlyn. *Silent Killers*. New York: Franklin Watts. 1988.

Graham, Frank, Jr., and Ada Graham. *Bug Hunters*. New York: Delacorte Press. 1978.

Graham, Frank, Jr. *The Dragon Hunters*. New York: Dutton. 1984.

Hunter, Beatrice Trum. "Monitoring Pesticides in Our Food." *Consumers' Research*. June 1989, p. 34.

Le Riche, W. Harding. *A Chemical Feast*. New York: Facts on File Publications. 1982.

Metcalf, Robert L. "Changing Role of Insecticides in Crop Protection." *Annual Review of Entomology*. 1980. 25:219–56.

Mettger, Zak, and Gary Moll. "IPM: Best Approach to Pest Control." *American Forests*. January/February 1989, p. 61.

Moore, Dr. John A. "NRDC Report Flawed." *Consumers' Research*. May 1989, p. 15.

Mott, Lawrie, and Karen Snyder. *Pesticide Alert*. San Francisco: Sierra Club Books. 1987.

Nielsen, Susan. "Pesticides and Fruit: Ways to Lower Your Risks." *Good Housekeeping*. June 1989, p. 241.

Pim, Linda R. *The Invisible Additives*. New York: Doubleday. 1981.

Pringle, Laurence. *Lives at Stake*. New York: Macmillan. 1980.

―――. *Our Hungry Earth: The World Food Crisis*. New York: Macmillan. 1976.

―――. *Pests and People*. New York: Macmillan. 1972.

Sampson, Neil. "Pesticide Breakthrough." *American Forests*. May/June 1988, p. 8.

Trost, Cathy. *Elements of Risk*. New York: Times Books. 1984.

Van Den Bosch, Robert. *The Pesticide Conspiracy*. Garden City, NY: Doubleday. 1978.

―――, and P. S. Messenger. *Biological Control*. New York: Intex Educational Publishers. 1973.

Yepsen, Roger B., Jr., Ed. *Organic Plant Protection*. Emmaus, PA: Rodale Press. 1976.

FOR FURTHER READING

Carson, Rachel. *Silent Spring*. Boston. Houghton Mifflin. 1962.

Fichter, George S. *Insect Pests*. New York. Golden Press. 1966.

Gay, Kathlyn. *Silent Killers*. New York. Franklin Watts. 1988.

Graham, Frank, Jr., and Ada Graham. *Bug Hunters*. New York. Delacorte Press. 1978.

Pringle, Laurence. *Lives at Stake*. New York. Macmillan. 1980.

Pringle, Laurence. *Pests and People*. New York. Macmillan. 1972.

Woods, Geraldine, and Harold Woods. *Pollution*. New York. Franklin Watts. 1985.

INDEX

Termites, 18, 86
Testing foods, 61–67
Toads as predators, 74
Tolerance by plants, 92
Tolerance Enforcement
    Program, 67
Tolerance level, 64
Topical residue, 60
Total Diet Study, 65
Toxicity tests, 62
Traps, 11, 86–88, 93–95,
    107, 109
2,4-D, 15, 33–34
Typhus and DDT, 12

Vacuum cleaners, 86
Vedalia beetles, 21, 40, 71,
73–74, 84
Vietnam, herbicides in, 15
Viruses, 23, 78–80

War, pesticides in, 15
Wasps, 76
Weather and pests, 72
Weeds, 22
    herbicides for, 33–34
    mechanical control of,
    87
    natural control of, 74–
    75, 104
White hellebore, 29
Wildlife
    and pesticides, 52–53
    as pests, 26

ABOUT THE AUTHOR

Sally Lee is a writer and former special education teacher. She has written numerous stories and articles for various young reader publications, including *Cricket, Teen,* and *Highlights for Children.* She is also the author of a number of books for Franklin Watts, including *Donor Banks, Predicting Violent Storms, The Throwaway Society,* and *New Theories on Diet and Nutrition.*

Mrs. Lee lives in Texas with her husband, Stephen, who is a petroleum engineer, and her two children, Michael and Tracy.